David Macbrayne

Summer Tours in Scotland

Glasgow to the Highlands

David Macbrayne

Summer Tours in Scotland
Glasgow to the Highlands

ISBN/EAN: 9783337331559

Printed in Europe, USA, Canada, Australia, Japan

Cover: Foto ©Andreas Hilbeck / pixelio.de

More available books at **www.hansebooks.com**

OFFICIAL GUIDE.
NEW EDITION.
1886.

SUMMER TOURS IN SCOTLAND.

GLASGOW TO THE HIGHLANDS.

"ROYAL ROUTE."

(Via Crinan and Caledonian Canals.)

WITH TIME TABLES AND LIST OF FARES,

BY

DAVID MACBRAYNE'S

ROYAL MAIL STEAMERS,

"COLUMBA," "IONA," &c.

[ENTERED AT STATIONER'S HALL.]

SAILING BILLS PUBLISHED MONTHLY and sent FREE on application to
DAVID MACBRAYNE, 119 HOPE STREET, GLASGOW.

LIST OF CALLING PLACES WITH REFERENCE PAGE.

Place	Page	Place	Page	Place	Page
Abriachan,	50	Gairlochy,	41	Loch Sunart,	62
Aldourie,	51	Gigha,	83	Loch Torridon,	91
Appin,	35	Glasgow,	17	Luing,	29
Applecross,	75	Glencoe,	74	Mallaig,	91
Ardlamont,	23	Glenelg,	67	Oban,	32
Ardpatrick,	83	Greenock,	20	Oldney,	75
Ardrishaig,	25	Harris,	95	Partick Wharf,	17
Ardgour Pier,	37	Innellan,	21	Plockton,	102
Arisaig,	93	Inveraray,	21	Poolewe,	99
Armadale,	67	Inverfarigaig,	43	Port-Askaig,	83
Aultbea,	99	Inverie,	91	Port-Charlotte,	83
Badcall,	75	Invermorriston,	47	Port-Ellen,	86
Ballachulish,	36	Inverness,	51	Portree,	70
Balmacara,	68	Iona,	59	Port-Sonnachan,	79
Banavie,	38	Islay,	80	Princes Pier,	20
Broadford,	69	Isleornsay,	67	Raasay,	101
Bruchladich,	83	Jeantown,	102	Rothesay,	22
Cairndaan,	27	Jura,	90	Salen, L. Sunart,	106
Carsaig,	61	Kilchoan,	106	Salen, Mull,	55
Clachan,	83	Kirn,	21	Skipness,	24
Colintraive,	22	Kyleakin,	68	Staffa,	57
Corpach,	38	Kyles of Bute,	23	Stornoway,	100
Corran,	37	Laggan,	42	Strome Ferry,	102
Craignish,	28	Lismore,	74	Strontian,	106
Craignure,	55	Lochaline,	55	Tanera,	91
Crinan,	28	Lochawe,	73	Tarbert, Harris,	95
Cullochy,	44	Loch Carron,	102	Tarbert, Lochfyne,	24
Dunmore,	83	Loch Coruisk,	65	Temple Pier,	49
Dunoon,	21	Loch Duich,	91	Thurso,	75
Easdale,	30	Loch Eribol,	75	Tighnabruaich,	23
Eigg,	63	Loch Inchard,	75	Tobermory,	56
Ford,	79	Loch Inver,	97	Tongue,	75
Fort-Augustus,	44	Loch Maddy,	94	Totaig,	91
Fort-William,	37	Loch Maree,	72	Ullapool,	96
Foyers,	47	Lochnevis,	91	Urquhart,	49
Gairloch,	71	Loch Scavaig,	65	West Loch Tarbert,	81

Return Tickets as undernoted are issued on board Columba, Iona, or other Steamer

RETURN FARES. Available during the season	From Glasgow.		From Greenock.		Kirn, Dunoon, or Innellan.		From Rothesay.		From Tigh'bruaich	
TO	Cabin.	Steer.	Cabin.	Steer.	Cabin.	Steer.	Cabin.	Steer.	Cabin	Steer.
	s. d.	s. d.	s. d.	s. d.	s. d.	s. d.	s. d.	s. d.	s. d.	s. d.
Kirn, Dunoon or Innellan,	2 0	1 6	1 0							
Rothesay,	2 6	1 6	1 9	1 3	1 0	1 0				
Colintraive,	3 6	2 6	3 0	2 0	2 0	1 6	1 0	1 0		
Tighnabruaich	3 6	2 6	3 0	2 0	2 0	1 6	1 6	1 0		
*Tarbert,	6 0	3 6	5 0	3 0	4 0	2 6	3 0	2 0	2 0	1 3
*Ardrishaig,	6 0	3 6	5 0	3 0	4 0	2 6	3 6	2 0	2 6	1 6

The Places marked thus * are for Day of Issue only, Friday and Saturday's issue of Tickets available till Monday.

CONTENTS.

	PAGE
GLASGOW TO ARDRISHAIG, OBAN, BANAVIE, AND INVERNESS,	17
Do., ,, OBAN via LOCHAWE,	78
Do., ,, ISLAY via TARBERT,	80
Do., ,, STORNOWAY via MULL OF KINTYRE,	91
Do., ,, THURSO via MULL OF KINTYRE,	75
Do., ,, INVERNESS AND BACK via MULL OF KINTYRE,	108
OBAN TO STAFFA AND IONA,	54
Do., ,, MULL, SKYE, AND GAIRLOCH,	62
Do., ,, GLENCOE, FORT-WILLIAM, AND CORPACH,	74
Do., ,, INVERNESS,	32
Do., ,, LOCHAWE,	106
PORTREE TO STORNOWAY via LOCHMADDY AND TARBERT (HARRIS),	94
Do., ,, do., ,, ULLAPOOL AND LOCHINVER,	96
Do., ,, do., ,, GAIRLOCH, POOLEWE, AND AULTBEA,	98
Do., ,, do., DIRECT,	99
Do., TO STROME FERRY AND INVERNESS, via RAASAY, BROADFORD, ETC.,	101
Do., TO INVERNESS via ULLAPOOL AND GARVE,	102
STORNOWAY TO INVERNESS (MAIL ROUTE) via STROME FERRY,	101
LIST OF FARES FROM GLASGOW,	5
Do. AND CIRCULAR TOURIST TICKETS,	6
Do. FROM OBAN,	8
TIME TABLE :—THROUGH ROUTE TO INVERNESS,	16
Do. GLASGOW TO OBAN via LOCHAWE,	78
Do. OBAN TO STAFFA AND IONA,	54
Do. do. MULL, SKYE, AND GAIRLOCH,	62
Do. do. BALLACHULISH, FORT-WILLIAM, AND CORPACH,	74

LIST OF ILLUSTRATIONS,

(In the Sixpenny and One Shilling Guide Book.)

	Facing Page
MAP OF DAVID MACBRAYNE'S STEAMERS' ROUTES,	
KYLES OF BUTE, AT GLEN CALADH,	22
TARBERT (LOCHFYNE) FROM THE SOUTH,	24
OBAN, FROM THE SOUTH,	32
THE CALEDONIAN CANAL AT FORT-AUGUSTUS,	44
INVERNESS, FROM THE CASTLE,	52
ISLAND OF STAFFA.	56
FINGAL'S CAVE, STAFFA,	58
IONA CATHEDRAL AND ST. ORAN'S CHAPEL,	60
LOCH CORUISK, SKYE,	66
FLOWERDALE, GAIRLOCH, ROSS-SHIRE,	72
HANDA, ISLAND,	74
THURSO,	76
PASS OF BRANDER, LOCHAWE,	78

SUMMER TOURS IN SCOTLAND.
THE ROYAL ROUTE.
GLASGOW AND THE HIGHLANDS
Via Crinan and Caledonian Canals.

TOURISTS SPECIAL Cabin Tickets issued during the Season, Giving the *privilege* of the run of *all the undernamed Steamers to any part of the Highlands* at which they may call during the time specified.

For One Week, £3; Two Weeks, £5; or Six Separate Days, £3 10.

NEW ROYAL MAIL STEAM SHIP "GRENADIER."

Columba	Mountaineer	Claymore	Islay
Iona	Pioneer	Clansman	Lochiel
Chevalier	Lochawe	Clydesdale	Fingal
Gondolier	Glencoe	Cavalier	Lochness. Ethel
Glengarry	Linnet	Staffa.	Inveraray Castle

THE ROYAL MAIL SWIFT PASSENGER STEAMER
"COLUMBA" OR "IONA"

Sails daily from May till October, from Glasgow at 7 A.M., and from Greenock about 9 A.M., in connection with Express Trains from London and the South, Edinburgh, and Glasgow, &c., for KYLES OF BUTE, TARBERT, and ARDRISHAIG, conveying Passengers for OBAN, GLENCOE, INVERNESS, LOCHAWE, STAFFA and IONA, MULL, SKYE, GAIRLOCH, STORNOWAY, THURSO, &c., &c.

Dining, Refreshment and other accommodation provided for Cabin and 1st Class Passengers in Saloon, and for Steerage and 3rd Class Passengers in Fore Cabin. Any Steerage or 3rd Class Passengers found using Saloon for any purpose whatever will be charged Cabin Passage Money.

A WHOLE DAY'S SAIL BY THE "COLUMBA" OR "IONA,"
From Glasgow to Ardrishaig and Back (180 miles)

CABIN FARE, ... 6/. or including Breakfast, Dinner and Tea 12/.
FORE CABIN FARE, ... 3/6. do. do., do. do. 7/.

TOURS TO THE WEST HIGHLANDS,
(Occupying about a week.)
BY STEAM SHIP
"CLAYMORE" or "CLANSMAN,"

Via Mull of Kintyre, going and returning through the Sounds of Jura, Mull, and Skye, calling at Oban, Tobermory, Portree, STORNOWAY, and intermediate places.

CABIN RETURN FARE, 45s.

The Route is through scenery rich in historical interest and unequalled for grandeur and variety These vessels leave Glasgow every Monday and Thursday about 12 noon, and Greenock about 5 p.m., returning from Stornoway every Monday and Wednesday.
Breakfast, Dinner, and Tea, 7s. per Day.
Passengers continuing the voyage to THURSO and back pay 10s. extra fare.

The Steam-Ship **CAVALIER** or **STAFFA** will leave Glasgow every Monday and Thursday at 11 a.m. and Greenock at 4 p.m., for Inverness and Back, (via Mull of Kintyre) leaving Inverness every Monday and Thursday morning; Cabin Fare for the Trip, with First-class Sleeping Accommodation, 30/; or including Meals, by Steamer leaving Glasgow on Mondays 60/, on Thursday 65/.

OFFICIAL GUIDE BOOK, 3D.; ILLUSTRATED, 6D.; CLOTH GILT, 1s
Time Bill, Map and List of Fares, sent free on application to the Owner,

DAVID MACBRAYNE, 119 HOPE STREET, GLASGOW.

SWIFT STEAMERS TOURIST FARES FROM GLASGOW.

Tickets as undernoted are issued on board "Columba," "Iona," or other Steamers, available during season, with permission to break journey at any place on the route.

FROM GLASGOW TO	Single Via Crinan Cabin	Single Via Crinan Steer.	Return Via Crinan Cabin.	Return Via Crinan Steer.	Return Cabin and 1st Cl.	Return Cabin and 3rd Cl.	Return Steer. and 3rd Cl.	Single Via Lochawe Cabin.	Single Via Lochawe Steer.	Going via Lochawe Return via Crinan or vice versa Cabin.	Going via Lochawe Return via Crinan or vice versa Steer.
	s. d.	s. d.	s. d.	s. d.				s. d.	s. d.	s. d.	s. d.
Colintraive	2 0	1 6	3 6	2 6	Going via Crinan, Returning from Oban by Railway via Callander.			Coachman's Fee Included.	Cabin of Lochawe Steamer and Coachman's Fee included.	Coachman's Fee Included.	Cabin of Lochawe Steamer and Coachman's Fee included.
Tighnabruaich	2 6	1 6	3 6	2 6							
Tarbert	4 6	2 6	6 9	4 0							
Ardrishaig	5 0	2 6	7 6	4 0							
Crinan	8 0	4 0	12 0	6 6							
Craignish	10 0	5 0	15 0	8 0							
Luing	11 0	5 6	17 0	8 6							
Easdale	12 6	6 0	19 0	9 6							
Islay	12 6	5 0	19 0	8 6	s. d.	s. d.	s. d.				
Oban	13 0	7 6	20 0	11 0	21 0	16 0	11 6	17 6	13 0	22 6	17 6
do. Valid Frid. or Sat. till Mon.			18 0	10 0	18 0	14 6	10 0				
Appin	15 0	8 6	23 0	13 0	24 0	19 0	14 0	19 6	14 0	25 6	19 6
Ballachulish, Corran	18 0	9 6	27 6	14 6	28 6	23 6	16 0	22 6	15 0	30 0	21 0
Fort-William, Corpach	20 0	10 6	30 0	16 0	31 6	26 6	17 6	24 6	16 0	33 0	22 6
Banavie	21 0		32 0		33 0	28 0		25 6		34 6	
Gairlochy	22 6	11 6	34 6	17 6	35 6	30 6	19 6	27 0	17 0	37 0	24 0
Laggan	25 6	12 6	39 0	19 0	40 0	35 0	21 6	30 0	18 0	41 6	25 6
Cullochy	27 6	13 0	42 0	19 6	43 0	38 0	22 6	32 0	18 6	44 6	26 0
Fort-Augustus	28 0	13 0	43 0	19 6	44 0	39 0	23 0	32 6	18 6	45 6	26 0
Invermoriston	29 6	13 6	45 6	20 6	46 6	41 6	24 0	34 0	19 0	48 0	27 0
Foyers	30 6	14 0	47 0	21 0	48 0	43 0	24 6	35 0	19 6	49 6	27 6
Inverfarigaig	31 0	14 6	47 6	22 0	48 6	43 6	24 6	35 6	20 0	50 0	28 6
Temple Pier	32 6	15 0	49 0	22 6	51 0	46 0	25 6	37 0	20 6	52 6	29 0
Inverness	33 6	15 0	50 0	22 6	53 0	48 0	26 6	38 0	20 6	54 6	29 0
Craignure	15 0	8 6	23 0	12 6	24 0	19 0	13 0	19 6	14 0	25 6	19 0
Lochaline	16 0	9 0	24 6	13 6	25 6	20 6	14 0	20 6	14 6	27 0	20 0
Salen (Mull)	17 0	9 6	26 0	14 0	27 0	22 0	14 6	21 6	15 0	28 6	20 6
Tobermory	18 0	10 0	27 6	15 0	28 6	23 6	15 6	22 6	15 6	30 0	21 6
Arisaig	23 0	12 6	34 6	18 6	36 0	31 0	19 0	27 6	18 0	37 6	25 0
Armadale	25 0	13 6	37 6	20 0	39 0	34 0	22 0	29 6	19 0	40 6	26 6
Isle Ornsay	25 6	14 0	38 6	21 0	40 6	35 6	23 6	30 0	19 6	42 0	27 6
Glenelg	26 0	14 6	39 0	21 6	42 0	37 0	25 0	30 6	20 0	43 6	28 0
Balmacara	27 0	15 6	40 6	23 0	45 0	40 0	26 6	31 6	21 0	46 6	29 0
Kyleakin	27 0	16 0	40 6	24 0	46 0	41 6	28 0	31 6	21 6	48 0	30 6
Broadford	28 0	16 6	42 0	24 6	48 0	43 0	30 6	32 6	22 0	49 6	31 0
Raasay, Portree	30 0	17 0	45 0	25 6	51 0	46 0	30 6	34 6	22 6	52 6	32 0
Gairloch, Strome Ferry	35 0	21 0	52 6	31 6				39 6	26 6	60 0	38 0

By Swift Steamer to Oban, thence per Claymore, Clansman or Clydesdale.

Arisaig	20 0		31 0		34 6	29 6		24 6		36 0	
Armadale	22 0		33 0		37 6	32 6		26 6		39 0	
Isle Ornsay	22 6		34 0		37 6	32 6		27 0		39 0	
Glenelg	23 0		35 0		39 0	34 0		27 6		40 6	
Balmacara	24 0		36 0		40 6	35 6		28 6		42 0	
Kyleakin	24 0		36 0		42 0	37 0		28 6		43 6	
Broadford	25 0		38 0		43 6	38 6		29 6		45 0	
Raasay, Portree	26 0		40 0		45 0	40 0		30 6		46 6	
Gairloch, Stornoway	32 0		48 0		52 6	47 6		36 6		54 0	
Lochinver, Ullapool, Lochmaddy, Tarbert (Har.)	34 0		51 0		52 6	47 6		38 6		54 0	
Thurso	37 0		58 0		62 6	57 6		41 6		64 0	

Passengers must fix by which route they wish to travel at the time of booking.
Children above 3 and under 12 years of age *half fare.*

CIRCULAR TOURIST TICKETS in connection with Caledonian Railway Co., are issued on board the "*COLUMBA*," "*IONA*," or other Steamer, as under, available during Season, with liberty to Break Journey at any Station on the Route.

No. of Tour.		Cabin & 1st Class.	Cabin & 3rd Class.	Steer. & 3rd Class
9	Glasgow to Ardrishaig, Ford, Lochawe, Callander and Glasgow,	20s. 0d.	17s. 6d.	15s. 6d.
9 B.	Do. do. do. and Edinburgh,	25s. 0d.	20s. 0d.	17s. 0d.
14	Glasgow to Oban (*via* Crinan), Oban to Callander and Glasgow,	21s. 0d.	16s. 0d.	11s. 6d.
14 C.	Do. do. valid Frid. or Sat. till Monday only,	18s. 0d.	14s. 6d.	10s. 0d.
14 B.	Do. do. Oban to Callander and Edinburgh,	25s. 9d.	18s. 4d.	13s. 10.
15	Do. do. Fort-William, Callander, & Glasgow,	52s. 0d.	49s. 0d.	30s. 6d.
15 B.	Do. do. and Edinburgh,	59s. 0d.	47s. 6d.	38s. 0d.
22	Glasgow to Portree & Gairloch & Back to Oban, & Rail to Glasgow,	51s. 0d.	46s. 0d.	34s. 0d.
60	Glasgow to Ardrishaig, Coach to Ford, Steamer on Lochawe, & Train to Oban, Returning (*via* Crinan) to Glasgow, or *vice versa*,	22s. 6d.	21s. 0d.	17s. 6d.

Any of undernoted Tourist Tickets can be made available via Lochawe, by paying on board "Columba" 6s extra.

64	Glasgow to Oban, (*via* Crinan) Crianlarich, Loch Lomond, Loch Katrine, Trossachs, Callander and Glasgow,	34s. 2d.	29s 2d.	24s. 8d.
64 B.	Glasgow to Oban (*via* Crinan) Crianlarich, Loch Lomond, Loch Katrine, Trossachs, Callander and Edinburgh,	39s. 0d.	31s. 6d.	27s. 0d.
65	Glasgow to Oban (*via* Crinan) Lochearnhead, Crieff and Glasgow,	29s. 0d.	22s 0d.	17s. 6d.
65 B.	Do. Do. Do. Do. and Edinr.,	33s. 9d.	21s. 6d.	20s. 0d.
68 B.	Glasgow to Oban (*via* Crinan) Oban to Crianlarich, Loch Lomond Balloch, Glasgow (Queen Street), and Glasgow (Central), to Edinburgh (Princes Street),	31s. 0d.	23s 6d.	19s. 0d.
69 B.	Glasgow to Oban (*via* Crinan), Oban to Callander, Trossachs, Loch Katrine, Loch Lomond, Balloch, Glasgow (Queen Street), and Glasgow (Central), to Edinburgh (Princes Street),	39s. 6d.	30s. 3d.	25s. 9d.
5 E.	Glasgow to Oban (*via* Crinan), Killin, Loch-Tay, Aberfeldy, Dunkeld, Perth & Glasgow, (available for one month only),	42s. 0d.	27s. 10d.	23s. 4d.
5 F.	Glasgow to Oban (*via* Crinan), Killin, Loch Tay, Aberfeldy, Dunkeld, Perth to Edinburgh (available for one month only),	41s. 0d.	26s. 6d.	22s. 0d.

No. of Tour.	Available for one month with permission to break journey anywhere, Glasgow to Inverness by Steamer, returning by Rail, via,	Cabin and 1st Class.	Cabin and 3rd Class.	Steerage and 3rd Class.
18	Keith, Aberdeen, Perth, and Stirling to Glasgow,	61/9	47/3	22/3
18 B	Do. do. do. Edinburgh,	60/0	45/11	30/11
18 C	Do. do. do. do. and Glasgow,	65/6	48/5	33/5
19	Blair-Athole, Pitlochry, Dunkeld, Perth & Stirling to Glasgow,	61/9	47/3	32/3
19 B	Do. Pitlochry, Dunkeld, Perth and Stirling to Edinburgh,	60/0	45/11	30/11
19 C	Do. do. do. do. Edinr. & Glas.	65/6	48/5	33/5
37 B	Aberdeen, Ballater, Braemar, Blairgowrie, and Perth to Glasgow,	77/4	Not yet in operation.	
37 C	Aberdeen, Ballater, Braemar, Blairgowrie, and Perth to Edinr.	77/1		

GLASGOW to SKYE and GAIRLOCH TOUR,

By Steamer to Portree & Gairloch (*via* Loch Maree) Coach and Rail to

		Cabin & 1st Class	Cabin & 3rd Class
23	—Inverness, Perth, and Stirling to Glasgow,	81s. 3d.	63s. 6d.
24	— Do. do. to Edinburgh,	82s. 9d.	61s. 3d.
23 B.—	Do do. to Edinburgh and Glasgow,	88s. 3d.	64s 8d.

Passengers may travel via STROME FERRY instead of via Lochmaree, *without extra charge*.

The Trip from **Oban to Staffa and Iona and Back**, can be combined with any of the Tours noted on pages 5, 6 & 7 on payment of 15/ additional.

TOURIST, THROUGH, & RETURN TICKETS are Issued on board the "COLUMBA" "IONA," or other Steamer, available any time during the Season, with permission to Break the Journey at any Place on the Route for **OBAN, STAFFA & IONA, LOCHAWE, LOCH LOMOND, LOCH KATRINE, TROSSACHS, BALLACHULISH, (GLENCOE), FORT-WILLIAM, BANAVIE, INVERNESS, PORTREE (ISLE OF SKYE), GAIRLOCH (LOCH MAREE), STORNOWAY, &c.**

	By Swift Steamers all the way.				By Swift Steamers to Oban, thence per Claymore or Clansman.	
	Single Cabin.	Single Strg.	Return Cabin.	Return Strg.	Single Cabin.	Return Cabin.
Glasgow to Oban (*via* Crinan), ..	13s. 0d.	7s. 6d.	20s. 0d.	11s. 0d.		
Do. do. do. Valid Frid. or Sat. till Mon.			18s. 0d.	10s. 0d.		
Do. do. (*via* Lochawe, ..	17s. 0d.	13s. 0d.	22s. 6d.†	17s 6d.†	† *Returning by Crinan.*	
Do. to Ballachulish (Glencoe),	18s. 0d.	9s. 6d.	27s. 6d.	14s. 6d.	—	—
Do. " Fort-William, ...	20s. 0d.	10s. 6d.	30s. 0d.	16s 0d.	—	—
Do. " Banavie, ...	21s. 0d.	..	32s. 0d.	..	—	—
Do. " Inverness, ...	33s. 6d.	15s. 0d.	50s. 0d.	22s. 6d.	—	—
Do. " Portree (Isle of Skye),	30s 0d.	17s. 0d.	45s. 0d.	25s. 6d.	26s. 0d.	40s. 0d.
Do. " Gairloch, ...	35s. 0d.	21s. 0d.	52s. 6d.	31s. 6d.	32s. 0d.	48s. 0d.
Do. " Stornoway, ...	..	..	..	..	32s. 0d.	48s. 0d.
Do. " Portree and Gairloch or Strome Ferry, and Inverness to Glasgow (*via* Caledonian Canal, &c.),			55s. 6d.	28s 6d.	Going via Lochawe Returning via Crinan Or vice versa.	60s 0d.
Do. " Stornoway, Mail Steamer to Strome Ferry, and Inverness to Glasgow (*via* Caledonian Canal, &c.),			60s. 0d.	31s. 6d.		64s. 6d.
					Cabin and First Class.	

SKYE and GAIRLOCH—(By Swift Steamers all the way). Via Lochawe,

		Return via Crinan 70/6	Returning via Crinan Or vice versa. 75s.
Tour No. 3 A.	By "Columba" Glasgow to Oban, Swift Steamer to Portree, & Gairloch, from Gairloch by Coach & Train to Inverness, & from Inverness by Str. *via* Caledonian Canal to Glasgow (or *vice versa*)		
Tour No. 2 A.	By "Columba" from Glasgow to Oban, Swift Steamer to Portree and Strome Ferry, Train to Inverness, and from Inverness by Steamer *via* Caledonian Canal to Glasgow, (or *vice versa*).	66/6	71s.
Tour No. 7 A.	By Steamers from Glasgow to Oban, Portree, and Ullapool, thence by Coach to Garve, and Train to Inverness, and from Inverness by Steamers *via* Caledonian Canal to Glasgow, (or *vice versa*),	70/6	75s.
NEW TOUR	By "Columba," "Claymore," or "Clansman," from Glasgow to Oban, Portree and Stornoway, from Stornoway by Mail Steamer to Strome Ferry, Train to Inverness, and from Inverness by Steamers *via* Caledonian Canal to Glasgow (or *vice versa*), ..	70/6	75s.

Valid One Month only.

CIRCULAR TOURIST TICKETS in connection with North British Railway Co., are issued on board the COLUMBA, IONA, or other Steamer, as under, available for One Month, with liberty to Break the Journey at any Station on the Route.

No. of Tour.	Any of the undernoted Tourist Tickets can be made valid via Lochawe, by paying on board Columba 6s extra.	CABIN and 1st Class.	CABIN and 2nd Class.	CABIN and 3rd Class.	STEERAGE and 3rd Class.
7	Glas. to Oban (*via* Crinan) Dalmally, Loch Lomond & Glas.,	37/3	—	32/6	23/
7C	Do. do. do. do. & Edin.,	42/9	—	35/	30/6
7B	Glas. to Ardrishaig, Lochawe, (Tarbet) Loch Lomond & Glas.,	35/11	—	—	—
	Glasgow to Inverness by Steamer, returning by Rail, via				
12	Dunkeld, Perth, Granton to Edinburgh and Glasgow,	65/6	55/8	48/5	33/5
13	Do. Dunblane and Larbert to Glasgow,	61/9	—	47/3	32/3
14	Do. and Granton to Edinburgh, ...	60/	51/9	45/11	30/11
15	Do. Dunblane and Larbert to Edinburgh,	60/	—	45/11	30/11
16	Keith, Aberdeen, Broughty, & Granton to Edin. & Glasgow,	65/6	55/8	48/5	33/5
18	Do. do. Dundee, Leuchars & Granton to Edinburgh,	60/	51/9	45/11	30/11
19	Do. do. do. Ladybank & Larbert to Edinburgh,	60/	—	45/11	30/11

GLASGOW to SKYE and GAIRLOCH TOUR, Cabin & 1st Class / Cabin & 2nd Class / Cabin & 3rd Class

By Steamer to Portree & Gairloch (*via* Loch Maree) Coach and Rail to

			Cabin & 1st Class	Cabin & 2nd Class	Cabin & 3rd Class
20	Inverness, Dunkeld, Granton to Edinburgh and Glasgow,	..	88s. 3d.	76s. 5d.	64s. 8d.
21	Do. do. Dunblane and Larbert to Glasgow,	..	84s. 3d.	—	63s. 6d.
22	Do. do. and Granton to Edinburgh, ...	..	82s. 9d.	72s. 6d.	61s. 3d.
23	Do. do. Dunblane and Larbert to Edinburgh,	..	82s. 9d.	—	61s. 3d.

Passengers may travel *via* STROME FERRY instead of *via* Loch Maree, *without extra charge*.
The Trip from Oban to Staffa and Iona and Back, can be combined with any of the Tours noted on pages 5, 6, and 7, on payment of 15/ additional

SWIFT STEAMERS' TOURIST FARES FROM OBAN.

Tickets as undernoted are issued on board all Mr. David MacBrayne's Steamers, available during Season, with permission to break journey at any place on the route.

FROM OBAN. TO	Single Cabin	Single Steer.	Return Cabin	Return Steer	Single Cabin	Return Cabin
	s. d.	s. d.	s. d.	s. d.	s. d.	s. d.
Appin,	2 0	1 6	3 0	2 6		
Ballachulish,	5 0	3 0	7 6	4 6		
Corran,	5 6	3 0	7 6	4 6		
Fort-William, Corpach,	7 0	4 0	10 6	6 0		
Banavie,	8 0	—	12 0	—		
Gairlochy,	9 6	5 0	14 6	8 0		
Laggan,	12 6	6 6	19 0	10 0		
Cullochy,	14 6	7 0	22 0	11 0		
Fort-Augustus,	15 0	7 6	23 0	11 6		
Invermoriston,	16 6	8 0	25 6	12 6		
Foyers,	17 6	8 6	27 0	13 0	Fares by Claymore, Clansman, or Clydesdale.	
Inverfarigaig,	18 0	8 6	27 6	13 0		
Temple Pier,	19 6	9 0	30 0	14 0		
Inverness,	21 0	10 0	32 0	15 0		
Craignure,	2 0	1 0	3 0	1 6	2 0	3 0
Lochaline,	3 0	1 6	4 6	2 6	3 0	4 6
Salen (Mull),	4 0	2 0	6 0	3 0	4 0	6 0
Tobermory,	5 0	2 6	7 6	4 0	5 0	7 6
Arisaig,	10 0	5 0	15 0	7 6	9 0	13 6
Armadale,	12 0	7 0	18 0	10 6	11 0	16 6
Isle Ornsay,	13 0	8 0	19 6	12 0	11 0	16 6
Glenelg,	14 0	9 0	21 0	13 6	12 0	18 0
Balmacara,	16 0	10 0	24 0	15 0	13 0	19 6
Kyleakin,	17 0	11 0	25 6	16 6	14 0	21 0
Broadford,	18 0	12 6	27 0	19 0	15 0	22 6
Rassay, Portree,	20 0	12 6	30 0	19 0	16 0	24 0
Gairloch, Strome Ferry,	25 0	15 0	37 6	22 6	21 0	31 6

By Swift Str. to Portree, thence Claymore, Clansman or Clydesdale.

Lochinver, Ullapool, Lochmaddy, Tarbert (Harris), Stornoway,	25 0	15 0	37 6	22 6	21 0	31 6
Thurso,	30 0	17 0	47 6	25 6	26 0	41 6

Oban to Ballachulish (for Glencoe), Cabin Return 7/6, and Fort-William, Cabin Return 10/6
Oban to Staffa and Iona (includes Landing, Guides, etc., at Staffa and Iona, 15/
Oban to Portree and Gairloch or Strome Ferry, and Inverness to Oban, 37/6
Oban to Stornoway, Mail Str. to Strome Ferry and Inverness to Oban, 42/

SKYE and GAIRLOCH—(By Swift Steamers all the way). Valid one month only.
Oban Tour No. 3 A.—By Swift Steamer from Oban to Portree and Gairloch, and from Gairloch by Coach and Train to Inverness, and from Inverness by Steamer *via* Caledonian Canal to Oban (or *vice versa*), Cabin and 1st Class 52/6

Oban Tour No. 2 A.—By Swift Steamer from Oban to Portree and Strome Ferry, Train to Inverness, and from Inverness by Steamer *via* Caledonian Canal to Oban (or *vice versa*), 48/6

Oban Tour No. 7 A.—By Swift Str. or Clansman Oban to Portree and Ullapool, thence by Coach to Garve, Train to Inverness, and from Inverness by Steamers *via* Caledonian Canal to Oban (or *vice versa*) 52/6

OBAN NEW TOUR.—By Swift Steamer or "Claymore," and "Clansman," from Oban to Portree and Stornoway, from Stornoway by Mail Steamer to Strome Ferry, Train to Inverness, and from Inverness by Steamers *via* Caledonian Canal to Oban (or *vice versa*), 52/6

Note.—Passengers going *via* Ballachulish, Banavie, and Inverness, and returning *via* Skye can procure Tourist Tickets as noted above on board the Oban and Fort-William Steamers.

LEAVING GLASGOW ON MONDAY.

The following Programme can be accomplished in ONE WEEK during July, August, and September, and the £3 Special Weekly Tickets *are available for any of the Routes:—*

Monday,	Glasgow to Oban, by Steamer "Columba" or "Iona" *via* Kyles of Bute, Ardrishaig, and Crinan (or if *via* Lochawe, Coach 5/. Train 3/8 extra).
Tuesday,	Oban to Gairloch,(Ross-shire) bySwift Steamer *via* Loch Scavaig and Portree.
Wednesday,	Gairloch to Inverness, by Coach (*via* Loch Maree) to Auchnasheen, and Rail to Inverness (Coach 7/6, Train 7/8 extra).
Thursday,	Inverness to Oban, by Steamers, *via* Caledonian Canal and Loch Linnhe.
Friday,	Oban to Staffa and Iona, and Back.
Saturday,	Oban to Glasgow, by Steamers *via* Crinan, Ardrishaig, and Kyles of Bute.

—OR—

Monday,	Glasgow to Oban, by Steamer "Columba" or "Iona" *via* Kyles of Bute, Ardrishaig, and Crinan, (or if *via* Lochawe, Coach 5/, Train 3/8 extra).
Tues., Wed., Thurs.,	Oban to Stornoway and Back to Oban, by Swift Steamer to Loch Scavaig and Portree, and from Portree by "Claymore" or "Clansman" to Stornoway and Back to Oban. Fare includes first-class sleeping accommodation on board "Claymore" or "Clansman" from Tuesday till Thursday.
Friday,	Oban to Staffa & Iona, or Oban to Ballachulish, Ft.-Wm. and Back
Saturday,	Oban to Glasgow, by Steamers *via* Crinan, Ardrishaig, and Kyles of Bute.

—OR—

Monday,	Glasgow to Oban, by Steamer "Columba" or "Iona" *via* Kyles of Bute, Ardrishaig, and Crinan (or if *via* Lochawe, Coach 5/, Train 3/8 extra).
Tuesday, Wednes.,	Oban to Stornoway, by Swift Steamer to Loch Scavaig and Portree, and from Portree by Steamer "Claymore" or "Clansman" to Stornoway. Fare includes first-class sleeping accommodation in "Claymore" or "Clansman."
Thursday,	Stornoway to Inverness, by Mail Steamer to Strome Ferry, and Train to Inverness (Train 11/11 extra).
Friday,	Inverness to Banavie, Fort-William, Ballachulish, or Oban.
Saturday,	Banavie, Fort-William, Ballachulish, or Oban to Glasgow, by Steamers *via* Crinan, Ardrishaig, and Kyles of Bute.

—OR—

Monday.	Glasgow to Oban, by Steamer "Columba" or "Iona" *via* Kyles of Bute Ardrishaig, and Crinan (or if *via* Lochawe, Coach 5/ ; Train 3/8 extra).
Tuesday,	Oban to Gairloch, by Swift Steamer to Loch Scavaig and Portree (Skye).
Wednesday,	Gairloch to Oban, by Swift Steamer *via* Portree and Sound of Mull.
Thursday,	Oban to Inverness, by Steamers *via* Loch Linnhe and Caledonian Canal.
Friday,	Inverness to Banavie, Fort-William, Ballachulish, or Oban.
Saturday,	Banavie, Fort-William, Ballachulish, or Oban to Glasgow, by Steamers *via* Crinan, Ardrishaig, and Kyles of Bute.

—OR—

Monday,	Glasgow to Oban, by Steamer "Columba' or "Iona" *via* Kyles of Bute, Ardrishaig, and Crinan (or if *via* Lochawe, Coach 5/, Train 3/8 extra).
Tuesday,	Oban to Stornoway, by Swift Steamer to Loch Scavaig and Portree, and from Portree by Steamer "Claymore" or "Clansman" to Stornoway.
Wednesday,	Stornoway to Portree—Fare includes first-class sleeping accommodation in "Claymore" or "Clansman" from Portree to Stornoway and Back.
Thursday,	Portree to Inverness, by Steamer to Strome Ferry, and Train to Inverness. (Train 11/11 extra).
Friday,	Inverness to Banavie, Fort-William, Ballachulish, or Oban.
Saturday,	Banavie, Fort-William, Ballachulish, or Oban to Glasgow by Steamers *via* Crinan, Ardrishaig, and Kyles of Bute.

☞ *The Special Weekly Tickets at £3 are available on board the Lochawe Steamer, and by "Claymore" or "Clansman" via Mull of Kintyre.*

☞ *Passengers from Inverness can remain over night at Ballachulish (for Glencoe), and join the Staffa and Iona Steamer at Oban next morning.*

LEAVING GLASGOW ON TUESDAY.

The following Programme can be accomplished in ONE WEEK during July, August, and September, and the £3 Special Weekly Tickets *are available for any of the Routes:—*

Tuesday, **Glasgow to Oban,** by Steamer "Columba" or "Iona" *via* Kyles of Bute, Ardrishaig, and Crinan (or if *via* Lochawe, Coach 5/, Train 3/8 extra).
Wednesday, **Oban to Staffa and Iona,** and Back.
Thursday, **Oban to Gairloch,** by Swift Steamer *via* Sound of Mull and Portree (Skye).
Friday, **Gairloch to Oban,** by Swift Steamer *via* Portree and Sound of Mull.
Saturday, **Oban to Ballachulish, Fort-William, or Banavie,** and Back, or remain at any of those places.
Monday, **Banavie, Fort-William, Ballachulish, or Oban to Glasgow,** by Steamers *via* Crinan, Ardrishaig, and Kyles of Bute.

——OR——

Tuesday, **Glasgow to Oban, Ballachulish, Fort-William, or Banavie,** by Steamer "Columba" or "Iona" *via* Kyles of Bute, Ardrishaig, and Crinan.
Wednesday, **Oban, Ballachulish, Fort-William, or Banavie, to Inverness.**
Thursday, **Inverness to Portree,** by Rail to Strome Ferry, and Steamer to Portree.
Friday, **Portree to Oban,** by Swift Steamer *via* Sound of Mull. [Train 11/11 extra.
Saturday, **Oban to Staffa and Iona,** and Back.
Monday, **Oban to Glasgow,** by Steamer *via* Crinan (or if *via* Lochawe and Ardrishaig Train 3/8, Coach 5/ extra.)

——OR——

Tuesday, **Glasgow to Oban,** by Steamer "Columba" or "Iona" *via* Kyles of Bute, Ardrishaig, and Crinan (or *via* Lochawe, Coach 5/ Train, 1st Class, 3/8 extra),
Wednesday, **Oban to Staffa and Iona,** and Back.
Thursday, **Oban to Portree,** by Swift Steamer *via* Sound of Mull.
Friday, **Portree to Inverness,** by Steamer to Strome Ferry, and Rail to Inverness. Train, 1st Class, 11/11 extra.
Saturday, **Inverness to Oban,** by Steamers *via* Caledonian Canal and Loch Linnhe.
Monday, **Oban to Glasgow,** by Steamer *via* Crinan (or if *via* Lochawe and Ardrishaig Train, 1st Class, 3/3, Coach 5/ extra.

——OR——

Tuesday, **Glasgow to Oban, Ballachulish, Fort-William or Banavie,** by Steamer "Columba" or "Iona" *via* Kyles of Bute, Ardrishaig and Crinan.
Wednesday, **Oban, Ballachulish, Fort-William, or Banavie to Inverness.**
Thursday, **Inverness to Gairloch,** by Train to Auchnasheen, & Coach (*via* Loch Maree) to Gairloch (Train 7/8, Coach 7/6 extra).
Friday, **Gairloch to Oban,** by Swift Steamer *via* Portree (Skye) and Sound of Mull.
Saturday, **Oban to Staffa and Iona,** and Back.
Monday, **Oban to Glasgow,** by Steamer *via* Crinan (or if *via* Lochawe and Ardrishaig, Train 3/8, Coach 5/ extra).

——OR——

Tuesday, **Glasgow to Oban,** by Steamer "Columba" or "Iona" *via* Kyles of Bute, Ardrishaig, and Crinan (or if *via* Lochawe, Coach 5/, Train 3/8 extra).
Wednesday, **Oban to Staffa and Iona,** and Back.
Thursday, **Oban to Gairloch,** by Swift Steamer *via* Sound of Mull, and Portree (Skye).
Friday, **Gairloch to Inverness,** by Coach (*via* Loch Maree) to Auchnasheen, and Rail to Inverness (Coach 7/6, and Train, 1st Class, 7/8 extra).
Saturday, **Inverness to Banavie, Fort-William, Ballachulish, or Oban.**
Monday, **Banavie, Ft.-Wm, Ballachulish or Oban to Glasgow,** by Steamers,

☞ *The Special Weekly Tickets at £3 are available on board the Lochawe Steamer, and by "Claymore" or "Clansman" via Mull of Kintyre*

☞ *Passengers from Inverness can remain over night at Ballachulish (for Glencoe), and join the Staffa and Iona Steamer at Oban next morning.*

LEAVING GLASGOW ON WEDNESDAY.

The following Programme can be accomplished in ONE WEEK during July, August, and September, and the £3 Special Weekly Tickets *are available for any of the Routes:—*

Wednesday,	Glasgow to Oban,	by Steamer "Columba" or "Iona" *via* Kyles of Bute, Ardrishaig, and Crinan, (or if *via* Lochawe, Coach 5/. Train 3/8 extra).
Thursday,	Oban to Staffa & Iona, or Oban to Ballachulish, Ft.-Wm, and Back.
Friday, } Satur., }	Oban to Stornoway, by Steamer "Claymore" or "Clansman," *via* Sound of Mull, and Portree, Skye, &c.
Mon., } Tues., }	Stornoway to Glasgow, by Steamer "Claymore" or "Clansman," returning from Oban *via Mull of Kintyre*.

—OR—

Wednesday,	Glasgow to Oban,	by Steamer "Columba" or "Iona" *via* Kyles of Bute, Ardrishaig, and Crinan (or if *via* Lochawe, Coach 5/. Train 3/8 extra).
Thursday,	Oban to Gairloch, by Swift Steamer *via* Sound of Mull and Portree (Skye).
Friday,	Gairloch to Oban, by Swift Steamer *via* Portree and Sound of Mull.
Saturday,	Oban to Staffa and Iona, and Back.
Monday,	Oban to Ballachulish, Fort-William, or Banavie, and Back, or remain at any of those places.
Tuesday,	Banavie, Fort-William, Ballachulish, or Oban, to Glasgow, by Steamers *via* Crinan, Ardrishaig, and Kyles of Bute.

—OR—

Wednesday,	Glasgow to Oban, by Steamer "Columba" or "Iona" *via* Kyles of Bute, Ardrishaig, and Crinan (or if *via* Lochawe, Coach 5/, Train 3/8 extra).
Thursday,	Oban to Staffa and Iona, and Back.
Friday,	Oban to Inverness, by Steamers *via* Loch Linnhe and Caledonian Canal.
Saturday,	Inverness to Gairloch, by train to Auchnasheen, and Coach (*via* Loch Maree) to Gairloch (Train 7/8 ; Coach 7/6 extra).
Monday,	Gairloch to Oban, by Swift Steamer *via* Portree and Sound of Mull.
Tuesday,	Oban to Glasgow, by Steamers *via* Crinan, Ardrishaig and Kyles of Bute.

—OR—

Wednesday,	Glasgow to Oban, by Steamer "Columba" or "Iona" *via* Kyles of Bute, Ardrishaig, and Crinan (or if *via* Lochawe, Coach 5/ ; Train 3/8 extra).
Thursday,	Oban to Gairloch, by Swift Steamer *via* Sound of Mull and Portree (Skye).
Friday,	Gairloch to Oban, by Swift Steamer *via* Portree and Sound of Mull.
Saturday,	Oban to Inverness, by Steamers *via* Loch Linnhe and Caledonian Canal.
Monday.	Inverness to Banavie, Fort-William, Ballachulish, or Oban.
Tuesday,	Banavie, Fort-William, Ballachulish, or Oban, to Glasgow, by Steamers *via* Crinan, Ardrishaig, and Kyles of Bute.

—OR—

Wednesday,	Glasgow to Oban, by Steamer "Columba" or "Iona" *via* Kyles of Bute, Ardrishaig, and Crinan (or if *via* Lochawe, Coach 5/. Train 3/8 extra).
Thursday,	Oban to Gairloch, by Swift Steamer *via* Sound of Mull and Portree (Skye).
Friday,	Gairloch to Inverness, by Coach (*via* Loch Maree) to Auchnasheen, and Rail to Inverness (Coach 7/6, Train 7/8 extra).
Saturday,	Inverness to Oban, by Steamers, *via* Caledonian Canal and Loch Linnhe.
Monday,	Oban to Staffa and Iona, and Back.
Tuesday,	Oban to Glasgow, by Steamers *via* Crinan, Ardrishaig, and Kyles of Bute.

☛ *The Special Weekly Tickets at* £3 *are available on board the Lochawe Steamer, and by* "Claymore" *or* "Clansman" *via Mull of Kintyre.*

☛ *Passengers from Inverness can remain over night at Ballachulish (for Glencoe) and join the Staffa and Iona Steamer at Oban next morning.*

LEAVING GLASGOW ON THURSDAY.

The following Programme can be accomplished in ONE WEEK during July, August, and September, and the £3 Special Weekly Tickets are available for any of the Routes:—

Thursday,	Glasgow to Oban, by Steamer "Columba" or "Iona" *via* Kyles of Bute, Ardrishaig and Crinan (or if *via* Lochawe, Coach 5/, Train 3/8 extra).
Friday, Saturday,	} Oban to Stornoway, by Steamer "**Claymore**" or "**Clansman**," *via* Sound of Mull and Portree (Skye), &c.
Monday,	Stornoway to Inverness, by Mail Steamer to Strome Ferry, and Train to Inverness (Train 11/11 extra).
Tuesday,	**Inverness to Banavie, Fort-William, Ballachulish, or Oban.**
Wednesday,	**Banavie, Ft.-Wm., Ballachulish, or Oban to Glasgow**, by Steamers.

—OR—

Thursday,	Glasgow to Oban, by Steamer "Columba" or "Iona" *via* Kyles of Bute, Ardrishaig, and Crinan (or if *via* Lochawe, Coach 5/, Train, 1st Class, 3/8 extra).
Friday,	**Oban to Staffa and Iona**, and Back.
Saturday,	**Oban to Gairloch**, by Swift Steamer *via* Sound of Mull and Portree (Skye).
Monday,	**Gairloch to Oban**, by Swift Steamer *via* Portree and Sound of Mull.
Tuesday,	**Oban to Ballachulish, Fort-William, or Banavie**, and Back, or remain at any of those places.
Wednesday,	**Banavie, Fort-William, Ballachulish, or Oban to Glasgow**, by Steamers *via* Crinan, Ardrishaig, and Kyles of Bute.

—OR—

Thursday	Glasgow to Oban, by Steamer "Columba" or "Iona" *via* Kyles of Bute, Ardrishaig, and Crinan (or if *via* Lochawe, Coach 5/, Train 3/8 extra).
Friday,	**Oban to Portree**, by Steamer "Claymore" *via* Sound of Mull.
Saturday,	**Portree to Inverness**, by Steamer to Strome Ferry, and Rail to Inverness. Train 11/11 extra.
Monday,	**Inverness to Oban**, by Steamers *via* Caledonian Canal and Loch Linnhe.
Tuesday,	**Oban to Staffa and Iona**, and Back.
Wednesday,	**Oban to Glasgow**, by Steamer *via* Crinan (or if *via* Lochawe and Ardrishaig Train 3/8, Coach 5/ extra.)

—OR—

Thursday,	**Glasgow to Oban, Ballachulish, Fort-William or Banavie**, by Steamer "Columba" or "Iona" *via* Kyles of Bute, Ardrishaig and Crinan.
Friday,	**Oban, Ballachulish, Fort-William, or Banavie, to Inverness.**
Saturday,	**Inverness to Gairloch**, by Train to Auchnasheen, & Coach (*via* Loch Maree) to Gairloch (Train 7/8, Coach 7/6 extra).
Monday,	**Gairloch to Oban**, by Swift Steamer *via* Portree (Skye) and Sound of Mull.
Tuesday,	**Oban to Staffa and Iona**, and Back.
Wednesday,	**Oban to Glasgow**, by Steamer *via* Crinan (or if *via* Lochawe and Ardrishaig, Train 3/8, Coach 5/ extra).

—OR—

Thursday,	Glasgow to Oban, by Steamer "Columba" or "Iona" *via* Kyles of Bute, Ardrishaig, and Crinan (or if *via* Lochawe, Coach 5/, Train 3/8 extra).
Friday,	**Oban to Staffa and Iona**, and Back.
Saturday,	**Oban to Gairloch**, by Swift Steamer *via* Sound of Mull, and Portree (Skye).
Monday,	Gairloch to Inverness, by Coach (*via* Loch Maree) to Auchnasheen, and Rail to Inverness (Coach 7/6, Train, 1st Class, 7/8 extra).
Tuesday,	**Inverness to Banavie, Fort-William, Ballachulish, or Oban.**
Wednesday,	**Banavie, Ft.-Wm., Ballachulish, or Oban, to Glasgow**, by Steamers.

☞ *The Special Weekly Tickets at £3 are available on board the Lochawe Steamer, and by "Claymore" or "Clansman" via Mull of Kintyre.*

☞ *Passengers from Inverness can remain over night at Ballachulish (for Glencoe), and join the Staffa and Iona Steamer at Oban next morning.*

LEAVING GLASGOW ON FRIDAY.

The following Programme can be accomplished in ONE WEEK during July, August, and September, and the £3 Special Weekly Tickets *are available for any of the Routes:—*

Friday,	**Glasgow to Oban,** by Steamer "Columba" or "Iona" *via* Kyles of Bute, Ardrishaig, and Crinan (or if *via* Lochawe, Coach 5/, Train 3/8 extra).
Saturday,	**Oban to Gairloch,** by Swift Steamer *via* Sound of Mull, and Portree (Skye).
Monday,	**Gairloch to Inverness,** by Coach (*via* Loch Maree) to Auchnasheen, and Rail to Inverness (Coach 7/6, Train, 1st Class, 7/8 extra).
Tuesday,	**Inverness to Oban,** by Steamers *via* Caledonian Canal and Loch Linnhe.
Wednesday,	**Oban to Staffa and Iona,** and Back.
Thursday,	**Oban, to Glasgow,** by Steamers *via* Crinan, Ardrishaig, and Kyles of Bute.

——OR——

Friday,	**Glasgow to Oban,** by Steamer "Columba" or "Iona" *via* Kyles of Bute, Ardrishaig, and Crinan, (or if *via* Lochawe, Coach 5/, Train 3/8 extra).
Saturday,	**Oban to Inverness,** by Steamers *via* Loch Linnhe and Caledonian Canal.
Monday,	**Inverness to Oban,** by Steamers *via* Caledonian Canal, Fort-William, and Ballachulish.
Tuesday, Wednes., Thurs.,	**Oban to Stornoway, and Back to Glasgow,** by Swift Steamer to Loch Scavaig and Portree, and from Portree by Steamer "Claymore" or "Clansman" to Stornoway and Back, returning from Oban *via* Mull of Kintyre to Glasgow. Fare includes first-class sleeping accommodation in "Claymore" or "Clansman" from Tuesday till Thursday night or Friday morning.

——OR——

Friday,	**Glasgow to Oban,** by Steamer "Columba" or "Iona" *via* Kyles of Bute, Ardrishaig, and Crinan (or if *via* Lochawe, Coach 5/, Train 3/8 extra).
Saturday,	**Oban to Staffa and Iona,** and Back.
Monday,	**Oban to Inverness,** by Steamers *via* Loch Linnhe and Caledonian Canal.
Tuesday,	**Inverness to Gairloch,** by train to Auchnasheen, and Coach (*via* Loch Maree) to Gairloch (Train 7/8 ; Coach 7/6 extra).
Wednesday,	**Gairloch to Oban,** by Swift Steamer *via* Portree and Sound of Mull.
Thursday,	**Oban to Glasgow,** by Steamers *via* Crinan, Ardrishaig, and Kyles of Bute.

——OR——

Friday,	**Glasgow to Oban, Ballachulish, Fort-William, or Banavie,** by Steamer "Columba" or "Iona" *via* Kyles of Bute, Ardrishaig and Crinan.
Saturday,	**Oban, Ballachulish, Fort-William, or Banavie, to Inverness.**
Monday,	**Inverness to Oban,** by Steamers *via* Caledonian Canal and Loch Linnhe.
Tuesday,	**Oban to Gairloch,** by Swift Steamer *via* Loch Scavaig and Portree (Skye).
Wednesday,	**Gairloch to Oban,** by Swift Steamer *via* Portree (Skye) and Sound of Mull.
Thursday,	**Oban to Glasgow,** by Steamers *via* Crinan (or if *via* Lochawe and Ardrishaig, Train 3/8, Coach 5/ extra).

——OR——

Friday,	**Glasgow to Oban,** by Steamer "Columba" or "Iona" *via* Kyles of Bute, Ardrishaig, and Crinan (or if *via* Lochawe, Coach 5/, Train, 1stClass, 3/8 extra.)
Saturday,	**Oban to Gairloch,** by Swift Steamer *via* Portree (Skye).
Monday,	**Gairloch to Oban,** Swift Steamer *via* Portree and Sound of Mull.
Tuesday,	**Oban to Staffa and Iona,** and Back.
Wednesday,	**Oban to Ballachulish, Fort-William, or Banavie,** and Back, or remain at any of those places.
Thursday,	**Banavie, Fort-William, Ballachulish, or Oban to Glasgow** by Steamers *via* Crinan, Ardrishaig, and Kyles of Bute.

☛ *The Special Weekly Tickets at £3 are available on board the Lochawe Steamer, and by "Claymore" or "Clansman" via Mull of Kintyre.*

☛ *Passengers from Inverness can remain over night at Ballachulish (for Glencoe), and join the Staffa and Iona Steamer at Oban next morning.*

LEAVING GLASGOW ON SATURDAY.

The following Programme can be accomplished in ONE WEEK during July, August, and September, and the £3 Special Weekly Tickets are available for any of the Routes:—

Saturday, Glasgow to Oban, by Steamer "Columba" or "Iona" *via* Kyles of Bute, Ardrishaig, and Crinan (or if *via* Lochawe, Coach 5/, Train, 1st Class, 3/8 extra).
Monday, Oban to Staffa and Iona, and Back.
Tuesday, Oban to Portree, by Swift Steamer *via* Loch Scavaig.
Wednesday, Portree to Inverness, by Steamer to Strome Ferry, and Rail to Inverness, Train, 1st Class, 11/11 extra.
Thursday, Inverness to Oban, by Steamers *via* Caledonian Canal and Loch Linnhe.
Friday, Oban to Glasgow, by Steamer *via* Crinan (or if *via* Lochawe and Ardrishaig Train, 1st Class, 3/8, Coach 5/ extra).

—OR—

Saturday, Glasgow to Oban, Ballachulish, Fort-William, or Banavie, by Steamer "Columba" or "Iona" *via* Kyles of Bute, Ardrishaig, and Crinan.
Monday, Oban, Ballachulish, Fort-William or Banavie, to Inverness, by Steamers *via* Loch Linnhe and Caledonian Canal.
Tuesday, Inverness to Gairloch, by Train to Auchnasheen, and Coach (*via* Loch Maree) to Gairloch, (Train 7/8, Coach 7/6 extra).
Wednesday, Gairloch to Oban, by Swift Steamer *via* Portree and Sound of Mull.
Thursday, Oban to Staffa and Iona, and Back.
Friday, Oban to Glasgow, by Steamer *via* Crinan, (or if *via* Lochawe, and Ardrishaig Train 3/8, Coach 5/ extra.)

—OR—

Saturday, Glasgow to Oban, by Steamer "Columba" or "Iona" *via* Kyles of Bute, Ardrishaig, and Crinan (or if *via* Lochawe, Coach 5/, Train 3/8 extra).
Monday, Oban to Staffa and Iona, and Back.
Tuesday, Oban to Gairloch, by Swift Steamer *via* Loch Scavaig and Portree (Skye).
Wednesday, Gairloch to Inverness, by Coach (*via* Loch Maree) to Auchnasheen, and Rail to Inverness (Coach 7/6, Train, 1st Class, 7/8 extra).
Thursday, Inverness to Banavie, Fort-William, Ballachulish, or Oban.
Friday, Banavie, Ft.·Wm., Ballachulish, or Oban, to Glasgow, by Steamers.

—OR—

Saturday, Glasgow to Oban, by Steamer "Columba" or "Iona" *via* Kyles of Bute, Ardrishaig, and Crinan (or if *via* Lochawe, Coach 5/, Train 3/8 extra).
Monday, Oban to Staffa and Iona, or Oban to Ballachulish, Fort-William and Back.
Tuesday, } Oban to Stornoway and Back to Oban, by Swift Steamer *via* Loch
Wednes.. } Scavaig to Portree, and from Portree by "Claymore" or "Clansman" to
Tuurs.. } Stornoway & Back to Oban. Fare includes first-class sleeping accomodation on board Claymore or Clansman from Tuesday till Thursday.
Friday, Oban to Glasgow, by Steamers *via* Crinan, Ardrishaig, and Kyles of Bute.

—OR—

Saturday, Glasgow to Oban, by Steamer "Columba" or "Iona" *via* Kyles of Bute, Ardrishaig, and Crinan (or if *via* Lochawe, Coach 5/, Train 3/8 extra).
Monday, Oban to Staffa and Iona, and Back.
Tuesday, Oban to Gairloch, by Swift Steamer *via* Loch Scavaig and Portree (Skye).
Wednesday, Gairloch to Oban, by Swift Steamer *via* Portree and Sound of Mull.
Thursday, Oban to Ballachulish, Fort-William, or Banavie, and Back. or remain at any of those places.
Friday, Banavie, Fort-William, Ballachulish, or Oban to Glasgow by Steamers *via* Crinan, Ardrishaig, and Kyles of Bute.

☞ *The Special Weekly Tickets at £3 are available on board the Lochawe Steamer, and by "Claymore" or "Clansman" via Mull of Kintyre.*

☞ *Passengers from Inverness can remain over night at Ballachulish (for Glencoe), and join the Staffa and Iona Steamer at Oban next morning.*

From OBAN.

The following Programme can be accomplished in ONE WEEK during July, August, and September, and the £3 **Special Weekly Tickets** *are available for any of the Routes :—*

Leaving Oban on Mondays, Wednesdays, and Fridays.

Sundays excepted.
- 1st day. Oban to Staffa and Iona, and Back.
- 2nd „ Oban to Gairloch, by Swift Steamer *via* Sound of Mull, and Portree (Skye).
- 3rd „ Gairloch to Oban, by Swift Steamer *via* Portree and Sound of Mull.
- 4th „ Oban to Ballachulish, by Steamer (see Glencoe) and proceed to Banavie.
- 5th „ Banavie to Inverness, by Steamer *via* Caledonian Canal.
- 6th „ Inverness to Oban, by Steamers, *via* Caledonian Canal, Banavie, Fort-William, and Ballachulish.

―――OR―――

Sundays excepted.
- 1st day. Oban to Staffa and Iona, and Back.
- 2nd „ Oban to Gairloch, by Swift Steamer *via* Sound of Mull and Portree (Skye).
- 3rd „ Gairloch to Oban, by Swift Steamer *via* Portree and Sound of Mull.
- 4th „ Oban to Inverness, by Steamers *via* Loch Linnhe and Caledonian Canal.
- 5th „ Inverness to Oban, by Steamers *via* Caledonian Canal, & Fort-William, &c.
- 6th „ Oban to Lochawe and Back to Oban, by Steamer to Crinan and Ardrishaig, from Ardrishaig by Coach to Ford, and Steamer on Lochawe, thence by Rail to Oban, (Coach 5/, Train 3/8 extra).

EXTRA TOUR, leaving Oban on Tuesdays only.

- Tuesday, ⎫
- Wednes., ⎬ Oban to Stornoway and Back to Oban, by Swift Steamer to Loch Scavaig and Portree, and from Portree by "Claymore" or "Clansman" to Stornoway, and back to Oban. Fare includes first-class sleeping accommodation in "Claymore" or "Clansman" from Tuesday till Thursday.
- Thurs.,   ⎭
- Friday, Oban to Staffa and Iona, and Back.
- Saturday, Oban to Inverness, by Steamers *via* Loch Linnhe and Caledonian Canal.
- Monday, Inverness to Oban, by Steamers *via* Caledonian Canal, Banavie, Fort-William, and Ballachulish.

Leaving Oban on Tuesdays, Thursdays, and Saturdays.

Sundays excepted.
- 1st day. Oban to Gairloch, by Swift Steamer *via* Sound of Mull and Portree (Skye).
- 2nd „ Gairloch to Oban, by Swift Steamer *via* Portree and Sound of Mull.
- 3rd „ Oban to Ballachulish, by Steamer (see Glencoe) and proceed to Banavie.
- 4th „ Banavie to Inverness, by Steamer *via* Caledonian Canal.
- 5th „ Inverness to Oban, by Steamers *via* Caledonian Canal, Banavie, Fort-William, and Ballachulish.
- 6th „ Oban to Staffa and Iona, and Back.

EXTRA TOUR, leaving Oban on Fridays only.

- Friday,   ⎫ Oban to Stornoway, by Steamer "Claymore" or "Clansman," *via* Sound
- Saturday, ⎬ of Mull, and Portree (Skye), &c.
- Monday,   ⎫ Stornoway to Oban, by Steamer "Claymore" or "Clansman," *via* Portree
- Tuesday, ⎬ (Skye), and Sound of Mull.
- Wednesday, Oban to Inverness, by Steamers *via* Loch Linnhe and Caledonian Canal.
- Thursday, Inverness to Oban, by Steamers *via* Caledonian Canal—Banavie, Fort-William, and Ballachulish.

☛ *The Special Weekly Tickets at £3 are available on board the Lochawe Steamer, and by "Claymore" or "Clansman" via Mull of Kintyre.*

☛ *Passengers from Inverness can remain over night at Ballachulish (for Glencoe), and join the Staffa and Iona Steamer at Oban next morning.*

TIME TABLE.
GLASGOW, OBAN, FORT-WILLIAM AND INVERNESS.
SWIFT STEAMERS CARRYING PASSENGERS ONLY.

The following information is given for the convenience of Passengers, but the Proprietor **reserves the right of altering these arrangements** at any time he may find it necessary, and **does not guarantee the times stated below**.

The "**Columba**," "**Iona**," or other Steamer sails **daily**, from about middle of **May** till about middle of **October**, from Glasgow at **7 a.m.**, conveying Passengers daily for **Ardrishaig, Islay**, (via **Tarbert**), and **Oban** (via Crinan Canal). For **Fort-William** and **Inverness** every **Monday, Wednesday**, and **Friday** till about end of **June**; daily thereafter till about end of **September**; and every **Monday, Wednesday**, and **Friday** till about middle of **October**.

GOING NORTH.

	Daily A.M.
Glasgow ....leave	7 0
Partick Wharf ....,,	7 15
Greenock Custom House Pier..,,	9 0
Do. Prince's Pier........,,	9 5
Kirn................,,	9 25
Dunoon ....,,	9 35
Innellan ....,,	9 50
Rothesay ....,,	10 15
Colintraive .... { Kyles of } ..,,	10 40
Tighnabruaich { Bute } ..,,	10 55
Ardlamont,................,,	11 10
Tarbert................,,	12 0
Ardrishaig ....arrive	12 40p
Ardrishaig ....leave	1 0
Crinan ....arrive	2 55
Crinan ....leave	3 0
Craignish................,,	3 20
Luing ....,,	3 40
Easdale ....,,	4 0
Oban ....arrive	4 45

	Daily July Aug. Sept. A.M.	Daily P.M.	Mon. Wed. Fri. May June Oct. P.M.	Daily July Aug. Sept. P.M.
Oban......lea	6 0	12 45	4 50	4 50
Appin ....,,	6 40	1 30	5 25	5 25
Ballachulish ..,,	7 30	2 30	6 15	6 15
Corran ....,,	7 55	2 50	6 40	6 40
Fort-William ..,,	8 30	3 30	7 15	7 15
Corpach ....,,	9 0	3 50	7 30	7 30
Banavie ..arr	9 20	4 0	7 50 Tues. Stop	7 50

	Mon. Wed. Fri. May June Oct. A.M.	Daily A.M.	Tues. Thur. Sat. A.M.	Daily July Aug. Sept. A.M.
Banavie ..lea	9 30		8 0a	9 30
Gairlochy ....,,	10 30		9 0	10 30
Laggan ......,,	11 45	Daily A.M.	10 15	11 45
Cullochy ....,,	12 40p		11 15	12 40p
Ft. Augustus,	2 0	5 40	12 40p	2 0
Invermorriston ,,	2 30	6 10	1 10	2 30
Foyers ....,,	4 30*	6 45	2 30*	4 15*
Inverfarigaig ..,,	4 30	7 0	2 40	4 30
Temple Pier ..,,	5 0	7 30	3 0	5 0
Inverness arr	6 30	9 20	4 45	6 30

COMING SOUTH.

	Daily P.M.	Mon. Wed. and Friday. May, June, Oct. A.M.	Daily July Aug. Sept.
Inverness lea	3 0	..	7 0	7 0a
Temple Pier ..,,	4 45	..	8 30	8 30
Inverfarigaig ..,,	5 0	..	8 50	8 50
Foyers ....,,	5 15	..	9 50*	9 50*
Invermorriston ,,	5 50	..	10 20	10 20
Ft-Augustus.,	6 30	..	11 45	11 45
Cullochy ......,,		..	12 40p	12 40p
Laggan ......,,	Stop	..	1 45	1 45
Gairlochy ....,,		..	2 45	2 45
Banavie ..arr		..	3 0	3 30

	Tues Thur Sat May June Oct A.M.	Daily July, August September A.M.	Daily A.M.	P.M.
Banavie lea	4 45	4 45	8 45	3 35
Corpach ......,,	5 5	5 5	9 0	3 50
Fort-William ,,	5 15	5 15	9 20	4 0
Corran ....,,	5 45	5 45	10 0	4 35
Ballachulish ,,	6 5	6 5	10 20	4 55
Appin ......,,	7 0	7 0	11 20	6 0
Oban ..arr	7 40	7 40	12 15p	6 45

	Daily A.M.
Oban ......lea	8 0
Easdale.. ....,,	8 45
Luing ....,,	9 5
Craignish ....,,	9 30
Crinan ....arr	10 0
Crinan ....lea	10 0
Ardrishaig arr	12 15p
Ardrishaig lea	1 0
Tarbert ....,,	1 40
Ardlamont ....,,	2 20
Tighnabruaich..,,	2 40
Colintraive ....,,	3 0
Rothesay ......,,	3 30
Innellan ......,,	3 50
Dunoon ......,,	4 10
Kirn ......,,	4 15
Prince's Pier arr	4 45
Greenock ....,,	4 50
Partick Wharf..,,	6 30
Glasgow ....,,	6 45

In July, August & September, Passengers leaving Oban at 6 a.m., arrive at Inverness same evening.

*Passengers are usually allowed forty five minutes to visit the Falls of Foyers.

"THE ROYAL ROUTE."

GLASGOW TO INVERNESS,

Via Kyles of Bute, Ardrishaig, Crinan Canal, Oban, Ballachulish (Glencoe), Fort-William, Banavie, and Caledonian Canal.

ALSO TO

Staffa and Iona, Mull, Skye, Gairloch, Islay, Lochawe, Strome Ferry, Stornoway, &c.

GLASGOW TO ARDRISHAIG AND OBAN.

AS shown in the foregoing time table the far-famed Swift Passenger Steamer, "COLUMBA" or "IONA" sails during Summer from Glasgow every morning, (Sunday excepted), at 7 a.m., and from Greenock about 9 a.m., in connection with express trains from London, Liverpool, Manchester, Preston, Birmingham, Sheffield, Leeds, Bradford, York, Newcastle, Edinburgh, Glasgow, &c. The steamer can be overtaken at Greenock by trains which leave Glasgow about an hour later, but the sail down the river, will, on a fine morning (especially if it should happen to be high water), amply repay the tourist for getting up an hour earlier than is absolutely necessary.

<small>Glasgow</small>

The Harbour of Glasgow is fully two and a half miles long. As the steamer requires to proceed slowly while passing through, we can closely inspect the shipping on each side, and may observe the steamships of the "Anchor," "Allan," and "State" lines. On our left is the Kingston Dock; on our right the Queen's Dock, the construction of which occupied about ten years. Fifteen minutes after starting we arrive at our first stopping place, **Partick**, situated at the mouth of the Kelvin—a stream celebrated in Scottish song. Here we take on board passengers

<small>Partick</small>

from Govan (**on our** left) and others from the west-end of Glasgow. As the steamer proceeds, we have an excellent view of the shipbuilding yards on both sides of the river.

About two miles below Govan on the same side, is Shieldhall, and a little further down, on the right, Jordanhill, and Scotstown; whilst nearly opposite Scotstown, is the mansion of Elderslie. About thirty minutes sail from Glasgow brings us to Renfrew on the left bank of the river, one of the oldest burgh towns of Scotland, and which has the honour of giving a title to the Prince of Wales. After passing the pier we see Blythswood House (Sir Arch. Campbell, Bart), in the midst of a fine park, and surrounded by woods. A few miles from Renfrew, but distant from the river, is the village of Elderslie, in which is situated the reputed birth-place of Scotland's noblest hero, Sir William Wallace. The town of Paisley, with a population of 50,000, and noted for its woollen shawl manufactures, is about three miles up the river Cart. Opposite the junction of the river Cart with the Clyde, is the yard of Messrs. J. & G. Thomson, the builders of the "GRENADIER," "COLUMBA," and the three "IONA'S;" and on the same side, at Dalmuir, are the works of the Clyde Trustees.

The mansion we next pass, on the left, is Erskine House, erected by the late Lord Blantyre, who was accidentally killed at Brussels, during the insurrection of 1830. Up till the middle of the seventeenth century the barony of Erskine was the ancient patrimony of the Earls of Mar, who took their family name from it, when surnames began to be adopted in Scotland. The river here widens out somewhat, assuming the appearance of a lake, and the scenery is worthy of attention. The heights forming the background to the north are the Kilpatrick hills. The steamer now approaches, on our right, Bowling, a place which the passengers can easily distinguish by the numerous vessels laid up in its harbour. At Bowling, the entrance of the Forth and Clyde Canal, which unites the east and west coasts of Scotland, can be seen. This canal, 34 miles in length, was begun in 1768, and finished in 1790, at a cost of £330,000.

A little beyond "Bowling Bay," on a promontory, is

Dunglass Castle, and on a conspicuous part of the rock stands an obelisk erected to the memory of Henry Bell, who originated steam navigation in Europe. This ruined Castle was anciently a seat of the Colquhouns of Colquhoun and Luss, and is believed by some antiquaries to be the point at which the Roman Wall began, and which extended to Caeridden on the Firth of Forth, a distance of 36 miles. This rampart of earth rested on a stone foundation, and was upwards of 20 feet high and 24 feet thick.

Both sides of the river now are beautifully wooded, and trains can be seen passing to and fro on either side; the Greenock railway on the left, and the railway for Craigendoran (Helensburgh) and Lochlomond on the right.

The high hill to our right is Dumbuck, and before us is Dunbarton Castle which figures prominently as well as picturesquely in most of the many good views of the brilliant scenery of the upper reach of the Firth of Clyde. The rock rises to a height of 260 feet, and measures a mile in circumference; 16 cannons are mounted on it, but it has only a very small garrison. Ossian, speaking of "Balclutha" which signifies, the town of the Clyde, and which he is supposed to have used as a poetic name for Dunbarton Castle, says—

"The thistle shakes there its lovely head,"

and curiously enough the true Scottish thistle, though really a rare plant in Scotland, still grows wild it is said on Dunbarton Rock.

The river Leven flows into the Clyde here from Lochlomond, and a little beyond, on a fine sloping bank, stands the mansion house of Helenslee (Peter Denny, Esq.). At the junction of the Leven with the Clyde, by looking in a northerly direction, on an ordinarily clear day, Benlomond can be seen distinctly. About four miles below Dunbarton, on the same side, is Cardross; and about three miles nearer Dunbarton, on a wooded knoll forming part of the farm known as Castle Hill, stood a favourite residence of Robert the Bruce, in which he died in 1329. We next come in view, on our left, of the old Castle of Newark, a large quadrangular building, and then we pass Port-Glasgow, built in 1668, by the merchants of Glasgow. Since the river was deepened its importance has declined very much. The principal business now is shipbuilding and timber importing. Here the first steamer in Europe, the "Comet," was built.

Greenock   The second place of call is Greenock—Custom House Quay. Here we get our number of passengers increased; some from the London and North Western, and Caledonian Railways, and others from the town. Shipbuilding, engineering, and sugar refining, the principal trades of the town, are carried on very extensively, and the harbours and docks are thronged with vessels trading to all parts of the world. The population is about 60,000.

Prince's Pier   Leaving this the steamer makes for another calling place at Greenock, Prince's Pier, where we take on board other passengers who have come by train over the Midland, and Glasgow and South Western system. There is an extensive sandbank off Greenock, and this part of it, called the Tail of the Bank, is the best anchorage ground in the Firth of Clyde. Amongst the numerous vessels which we see "brought to" here, there is usually one of H. M.'s ships of war, and the anchorage is at intervals visited by the home squadron of H. M.'s ironclad fleet, when the sight is very imposing. Looking right across, Helensburgh, a favourite watering place, is to be seen, as also the entrance to the Gareloch, where a large number of vessels periodically get their compasses adjusted. On the shores of this loch stands Roseneath Castle, one of the seats of the Duke of Argyll.

Steaming off from Prince's Pier, the steamer glides swiftly along, passing the fine Esplanade at the west end of Greenock and the "Battery Point," on which is Fort Matilda, mounted with 7 guns. Towering above it can be seen the Sailors' Home, founded by Sir Gabriel Wood, a large and handsome building for aged and infirm merchant seamen. We next pass Gourock, the bay of which is a favourite anchorage for yachts. Gourock has easy access by tramway to Greenock, and many of the river steamers call at its pier. The west-ward, and fashionable part is called Ashton.

The scenery now increases in spaciousness, variety, and beauty—we have the Argyleshire hills in front Lochlong to our right, with the summer resorts of

Kilcreggan and Cove on the one side of it, Strone and Blairmore on the other, and the lofty Benlomond in the distance. As we proceed in the direction of the Holy Loch, looking out to sea on our left, a good view of Bute and the Islands of Cumbrae is to be had. In front of us the villas and cottages, which in the distance appear to be so closely built as almost to resemble a town, are, as the steamer nears the shore, found to be pretty wide apart and surrounded by green foliage, which gives them a most charming appearance.

Seventeen or eighteen minutes' sail from Prince's Pier (a distance of fully six miles,) brings us alongside Kirn Pier, which is our nearest landing place for Hunter's Quay, Sandbank, and other watering-places on the Holy Loch. In four minutes more we are at Dunoon, where passengers by Great Northern, North Eastern, and North British Railways, *via Craigendoran*, join the steamer. Dunoon is one of the oldest and most important watering places on the West Coast. At one time the only regular communication with Dunoon and the Renfrewshire shore, viz., the Highlands and Lowlands, was by the public Ferry. The green mound not far beyond the pier is surmounted by the remains of the Castle of Dunoon, formerly a royal residence. The highest hill in the background is Benmore, (2,500 ft.). Opposite Dunoon, is the "Cloch Lighthouse" erected in 1791. It is 80 feet high, and shows at night a light visible 12 miles off, and possesses a powerful fog-horn.

Passing the charming West Bay of Dunoon, and looking to the opposite shore, near the village of Inverkip, we see the mansion of Sir Michael Shaw Stewart, Bart., lord of the manor, and a little above Wemyss Bay, Castle Wemyss, the residence of John Burns, Esq., of the Belfast, Liverpool, and famous Cunard fleet. Below Wemyss Bay as we proceed, Skelmorlie and Largs are discernible on the Ayrshire side. The peaks of Arran may also be seen in front of us, but a much better view is to be had when we reach Lochfyne. Skirting along the "Bullwood" shore towards Innellan, our next calling place, we have a succession of very handsome villas situated amongst pleasant green sloping fields, studded with beautiful trees. On leaving Innellan we sail along the Cowal shore until we round Toward Point, on which there is a lighthouse. Beyond it to the right, is Castle Toward, pleasantly situated, the seat of A. S. Finlay, Esq. We now make for the Bute shore, and on our left in a southerly direction is Mount Stuart House, the seat of the Marquis of Bute. Upon the Bute shore we see numerous splendid summer residences, and after passing Craigmore Pier, and entering Rothesay Bay, the Hydropathic Establishment, and the Royal Aquarium are conspicuous.

Rothesay We now reach **Rothesay**. On the quay there is quite a crowd of people congregated; some to meet friends arriving, others for curiosity, and many who are bent on having a sail with us. Rothesay, the capital of Bute, is delightfully situated, and has a very mild climate. Rothesay Castle was a royal residence in the reign of Robert II. and his son Robert III., and the latter died there in 1406. The ruins are in excellent preservation. We next make for the entrance to the Kyles of Bute, and the scenery now becomes even more attractive than hitherto. On our left we pass Ardbeg point, and afterwards the bay and village of Port-Bannatyne, another watering place. To our right is Lochstriven (the "Rothesay weather-glass,") extending some nine miles inland, amongst huge hills. Before us towards our right is South Hall, (Col. Campbell). This estate is beautifully wooded; and the trees were so planted as to represent the positions of the British and French armies at the Battle of Waterloo; but as many of the trees have been lately cut down the effect is somewhat marred. The steamer next touches at

Colintraive **Colintraive**, the nearest landing place for Glendaruel. At this pier some groups of passengers leave us, mostly bent on having pleasant pic-nics on shore. Although few habitations are to be seen for miles around, there are many delightful walks, much frequented by those who are out on pleasure. Leaving Colintraive, we sail through the Kyles (or narrows) of Bute proper, and here the scenery increases in interest and beauty. The strip of water is very contracted, there being only a little more than sufficient width to allow our steamer to pass through between the mainland on our right and the

Island of Bute on our left. The tourist who for the first time sails through this strait is at a loss to know how the steamer can possibly proceed further, as the high steep hills in front seem to shut it entirely in, until he begins to notice an arm, as it were, of the sea to his right, and another to his left; but which one is likely to be taken is puzzling. The one to the right (Loch Ridden) extends six miles inland to Ormidale and Glendaruel. As the steamer turns to the left, Loch Ridden opens up in all its grandeur, and is indeed a sight well worth remembering. Here we have glen and mountain, loch and stream, with, if it be calm, the reflection of the hills in the bright green water, so that every turn we make discloses new and more exciting beauties. At the entrance to Loch Ridden is a little low island ("Eilan Greg") marked by a solitary tree. This was the scene of the failure of the Earl of Argyll's expedition in 1685, so graphically described by Macaulay. The castle we now pass is Glen Caladh, the property of George Robert Stephenson, Esq., C. E., of Newcastle, and nephew of the great engineer. The estate, since it came into Mr. Stephenson's possession, has undergone very considerable inprovement—what before was bare and barren, is now wooded and picturesque—no expense having been spared in beautifying the place, and adding to its natural charms. Almost directly opposite on the Bute shore are the "Maids of Bute," two rocks on a green spot upon the hill, resembling two maids sitting side by side. A few minutes more, after turning to our right at Rhubaan Point, we call at the pretty village of **Tighnabruaich**, an enjoyable sea-side retreat. Tighnabruaich is a Gaelic word, denoting "House of the Brae," as for a long time there was but one house here; of late, however, the place has increased very much. _{Tighna-bruaich.}

We next pass Kames, where there are large Powder Mills, but everything of an explosive nature is manufactured more than two miles from the shore on the road which strikes across to Lochfyne. Looking before us we see the low-lying island of Inchmarnock, and further off the Holy Isle. On this side of Ardlamont Point, or what is sometimes termed "Blind man's Bay," a ferry boat comes off to the steamer. On turning the point a good view is to be had of Ardlamont House situated to our right amongst beautiful trees. This mansion house is the seat of the chief of the Clan Lamont. In the distance away to the south, the island of Arran can be seen to advantage, with its loftiest mountain "Goatfell" towering 3000 feet above the sea. This island is twenty miles long from north to south, and ten miles broad from east to west. We are now in Lochfyne, and looking to our left, on a clear day, part of the Ayrshire coast is visible. The steamer is swiftly approaching the Kintyre coast, and the first place noticeable upon it is Skipness.

<small>Tarbert</small>

We next approach the natural harbour of East **Tarbert**, and call at the outside pier, which is half a mile from the village, and outside the harbour. Passengers returning same day have one hour and a half ashore, and (at a small charge) can drive to West Loch Tarbert or Escart Bay and back. From Tarbert there is all the year round, a daily coach to and from Campbeltown, as also coaches waiting to convey passengers and mails to the head of West Loch Tarbert, (the sail down that Loch is very fine), a distance of fully a mile, from which is a

<small>Islay *via* Tarbert see page 80</small>

daily swift steamer to and from Islay. This arrangement avoids the circuit of the Mull of Kintyre, and lessens the sea passage considerably. Tarbert, noted for its famous Lochfyne herring, was, not many years ago, little else than a fishing village, but recently a number of nice cottages have been built, and it is now a favourite resort, and is gaining in popularity every summer. From the variety of its picturesque scenery it has special attractions for artists, and is accordingly much resorted to by them. Overlooking the town is a fine old castle built by Robert the Bruce, and in which he resided in 1326.

After leaving Tarbert, Stonefield House (Colin G. Campbell, Esq.,) is seen before and after passing Barmore Island on our left; the situation of this house is equal to any we have yet noticed, being finely wooded for miles around. While we are steaming along the next four or five miles, and passing, still on the left, the small estate of Erins, and Inverneil, a good view may be had of the upper reach of Lochfyne, as far as Minard in the direction of Inveraray.

In a crescent-shaped bay before us is Lochgilphead, and as we approach, Kilmory Castle is seen to the right

of it, and **Ardrishaig** to the left. At Ardrishaig passengers for Oban and the North, land and proceed without delay to the Canal steamer "LINNET." Those passengers who have got their luggage properly labelled for the pier in the North at which they intend to land, need not trouble about seeing it forwarded, as this is done for them.

The "COLUMBA" returns from Ardrishaig about 1 p.m., on the arrival of the passengers from Oban and the North, and those who have come out for the day's sail have usually a short time on shore. The distance from Glasgow to Ardrishaig and back is about one hundred and eighty miles, and to any who have but one day to spare, it is impossible to find a lovelier trip or a more enjoyable route.

Ardrishaig.

ARDRISHAIG to OBAN and BANAVIE.

THE Crinan Canal, connecting Lochfyne with Loch Crinan, is nine miles long, and was constructed to enable vessels trading between the Clyde and the West Highlands to avoid the circuitous and, formerly considered, dangerous passage round the Mull of Kintyre. It was surveyed, and estimated for by Sir John Rennie the great civil engineer, and a Company, under the presidency of the Duke of Argyll, undertook its construction in the year 1793.

Unforeseen obstacles led to delay and financial embarrassment, and prevented the full execution of the works. It was however opened in an incomplete state in July, 1801. In 1805, and 1811, accidents occured to the embankments and reservoirs, and recourse had to be made to the Government for grants of money. These were finally expended in 1817 under the direction of Telford the celebrated engineer, and shortly afterwards the management of the Canal was taken over by the Caledonian Canal Commissioners, with whom it still remains. It has fifteen locks (the "LINNET" passes through nine only), and the summit level is supplied with water from eight lochs, situated about eight hundred feet high among the Knapdale Hills on the left bank. The last serious accident occured on the evening of the 2nd February, 1859, when the embankments of several of these lochs gave way, and the descending flood, rushing down the ravine through which the principal feeder flows and carrying in its course immense quantities of earth and boulders, filled the valley with many thousand tons of debris. Fortunately, on reaching the summit level, the flood divided, part flowing east and part west; and but for this circumstance, the injury to property—(there was no loss of life)—would have been more extensive than it was. The repairing of the damage caused by this accident cost about £16,000, and the Canal was re-opened on 1st May, 1860. For many years the swift passenger traffic was successfully conducted by means of a track-boat drawn by horses, ridden by postilions in brilliant scarlet uniforms; and our gracious Sovereign used this mode of conveyance when on her visit to the Highlands in 1847. In "Leaves from the Journal of our Life in the Highlands," Her Majesty says:—"The light on the hills was beautiful as we steamed down Loch Fyne. At five we reached Lochgilp, and all landed at Lochgilphead (Ardrishaig). We and our people drove through the village to the Crinan Canal, where we entered a most magnificently decorated barge, drawn by three horses ridden by postilions in scarlet. We glided along very smoothly, and the views of the hills—the range of Cruachan—were very fine indeed." To meet the requirements of an ever-increasing traffic, some years ago, the present elegant saloon steamer "LINNET" was built, which is capable of comfortably accomodating double the number of passengers that the old track-boat could.

The "LINNET" starts at 1 P.M. On the opposite shore of Lochgilp may be seen Kilmory Castle (Sir John P. Campbell, Orde Bart.), already noticed. Five minutes after leaving we pass, on the left, Glendarroch Distillery, situated at the foot of a nicely-wooded glen, and higher up the hill there is a pretty waterfall with a leap of fully one hundred feet. In a few minutes more we see on the right the town of Lochgilphead (over two thousand inhabitants), with the Argyll and Bute Combination Poor-house and Lunatic Asylum upon the hill behind. In the near foreground, are Bishopton Chapel and Palace, the seat of the Episcopal Bishop of Argyll and the Isles, built in 1851, and on the left the beautifully-wooded grounds, and ivy-covered mansion-house of Auchindarroch (Alexander Campbell, Esq.) Half-an-hour after leaving Ardrishaig we arrive at Cairnbaan (White Cairn), so called from a cairn that once stood here, and in which was discovered a cist, or stone coffin. In this neighbourhood are several "menhirs" or standing stones, and groups of "petroglyphs" or cup and circle sculptures, of great interest to the antiquary. At Cairnbaan, the entrance to the Vale of Dail, there is a series of locks (nine within a mile), and as the steamer takes about forty-five minutes to go through them, passengers generally prefer to walk the distance. At lock No 8—the last of the ascending series—traces of the devastation caused by the accident of 1859 are still plainly visible. On emerging from the valley and descending to the lower level on the west side, the Canal skirts the base of the Knapdale Hills, and to the right is the large plain or moss called Crinan Moss, about five thousand acres in extent. At the base of the hills bounding the plain on the north and east, can be seen the village of Kilmartin, and close by it the ruins of Carnasserie Castle; while on a clear day we here get a peep of the peaks of Ben Cruachan (3800 feet), sixteen miles east of Oban. Further off, still on our right, situated on the slope of a finely-wooded hill, is the noble mansion-house of Poltalloch, John Malcolm, Esq., whose extensive estate stretches for about forty miles in one continuous line. The mountains of Scarba and Mull are now seen in the distance. About fifteen minutes after leaving the lower lock the steamer reaches Bellanoch Bay, with the prettily-situated village of Bellanoch on its shore; and the right bank of the Canal is now bounded by the river Add and the waters of Inner Loch Crinan. In a few minutes we pass Kilmahumaig, where previous to the sixteenth century stood a fine chapel. The burying ground is still in use, and a little way to the left of it we get a glimpse of a green mound, crowned with a stone seat, from which, in the olden days, the Lords of the Isles were wont to dispense justice. A remarkable rock

Crinan

called the "Lion of Crinan," so named from its striking resemblance to a lion *couchant*, may now be observed on the right, while further off, situated on a bold promontory, is Duntroon Castle, a comparatively modern building erected upon the ruin of the ancient stronghold. We now arrive at Crinan, the western terminus of the canal, and leaving the "LINNET," half-a-minute's walk brings us to the pier, where we find either of the splendid steamships "CHEVALIER" or "IONA" waiting our arrival with steam up and ready to start. Immediately after going on board the Dinner bell rings for Cabin passengers, and as the strong sea air, which has been plainly perceptible for fully half-an-hour, whets one's appetite, the dinner is usually well patronised. (Steerage or Third-Class passengers dine in Fore Cabin about half-an-hour afterwards).

The mainland of Argyle, along the coast of which we here sail, is called Lorn, and is divided into two districts, Upper and Nether Lorn. The course of the steamer lies across the mouth of Loch Craignish, at the head of which may be seen, on our right, Barbreck House (Admiral Colin Campbell) and on our left we have the Sound of Jura, bounded on the east by the mountains of Knapdale and Kintyre, and on the west by the islands of Jura and Islay. The three conical mountains in the distance are the "Paps of Jura," about 2000 feet high. Some miles down the Knapdale coast we can see Downie House, where Thomas Campbell, the poet, spent some of his early student days. Fifteen minutes after leaving Crinan the steamer passes between the Point of Craignish and the Island of Garbreisha, by the "*Dorus Mor*," or Great Door, through which the tides run with a velocity of nearly eight miles an hour. Doubling the Point, we come in sight of Craignish Castle (Colonel Gascoigne), situated at the head of Loch Beg. The schistose rocks here claim the attention of geologists, being pierced in some places by trap-dykes, one of which, rising high above the surrounding strata, is often mistaken by tourists for a fragment of some feudal fortress.

Craignish

At Craignish a ferryboat generally comes out to the steamer. After leaving Craignish we have, on the left, a good view of the north end of Jura and the Island of

Scarba, between which is the celebrated whirlpool of Corryvrechan; while on a clear day may be descried the distant Colonsay. The Atlantic tide, rushing with prodigious velocity—about eighteen miles an hour—through the strait between Scarba and Jura, and impeded in its course by a great sunken rock that rises to within some fifteen fathoms of the surface, is thrown into such violent commotion that sometimes the roar of the waves can be heard at a distance of many miles. Corryvrechan shows to best advantage after a westerly gale, and with a flood tide, when the waves may be said to leap mountains high. The steamer is now crossing the mouth of Loch Melfort, and to the right is the Island of Shuna, bequeathed to the City of Glasgow for benevolent purposes by the late Mr Yeates. Rounding the Point of Luing we enter the Sound of Luing, with the Island of Lunga (J. M'Dougall, Esq.) on our left, and steaming along the coast for about three miles, arrive at **Black-Mill Bay, Luing.** The gable of the old mill from which the place takes its name, may be noticed standing close to the shore, and a little to the left is Ardlarach House (George Willison, Esq.), who farms the greater portion of the island, and whose steading—the model farm of the late Marquis of Bredalbane—is seen towards the right and further inland. Near Black-Mill Bay are three rocks remarkably alike, when looked at from a particular position, and called the *Cobblers of Lorn*. The tides here run strongly (about seven miles an hour), and at certain states the surface of the sea is covered with thousands of miniature whirlpools. We now pass Phladda Lighthouse and the Island of Belnahua, and to our right is the village of Collupool, where, as also on Belnahua, there are extensive slate quarries. A group of isles may be seen two or three miles to westward of the lighthouse, and on the summit of the northernmost—Dunconnel—are the remains of a large fortification. Connel crossed over from Ireland about the 11th century. The next island Garveloch, is the largest of the group. The southmost island in the chain *Eileacha Naombh* (*Anglice*, Holy Isle) is associated with the memory of St. Columba. About the middle of the island, and on its eastern shore, are the saint's landing place and well—a spring of delicious water. Near this are the remains of two specimens of the bee-hive structure; the ruins of a chapel; an underground cell of neat construction, and an old burying-ground with sculptured stones, which are fast disappearing beneath the untrodden soil. A little to the south of the burying-ground, on a sunny slope, there is a small stone circle with a cross rudely engraved on one of the stones. Tradition points to this spot as the burial-place of St. Columba's mother. For an interesting description of a visit to this island, see "Hinba," *Cornhill Magazine*, February, 1880.

We now sail for a short time on the waters of the broad Atlantic. To the left lies the Island of Mull—"Dark Mull"—with its bold, black bluffs and lofty mountains—Ben Mhor, Ben Buy, Ben Talla, and stretching away to the west the Ross of Mull, and low-lying Ardalanish Point; a few miles on the other side of which is Iona. On our right may be noticed the Strait or Sound of Cuan, separating Luing from the next island, Seil. Before us is Easdale, and at the head of the bay, on the right, are Dunmore House (Mrs. Gillies) and the Free Church Manse.

Shortly, by a very narrow and rocky channel, almost invisible till we are close upon it, the steamer glides between the Islands of Easdale (left) and Seil (right), and arrives at Easdale Pier. The village has a population of about 900; and the quarries, celebrated for the quality of the slates produced, are very extensive, affording employment to about 300 men and boys. They have been wrought for over 200 years, and are now sunk fifty fathoms below the level of the sea. In 1862 a serious accident—fortunately unattended by any loss of life— occurred by the sea breaking in and flooding one of the quarries. It took nearly three years to pump it out. The men are hardy, industrious, and intelligent, and are first-rate boatmen, while many of them are artillery volunteers, maintaining a high rate of efficiency.

We are now in the Firth of Lorn, and to our left, in the distance may be seen the entrance to the Sound of Mull; the Mountains of Morvern, and the southern extremity of the Island of Lismore, with its lighthouse; before us is the Island of Kerrera. Our course lies close

Easdale

to the coast of Seil, and a little way outside the harbour another very prominent trap-dyke may be observed. We pass on the left Sheep Island, and on the right, at Barnacarry Point is a curious rock, called from its resemblance to a squat frog—the Frog of Lorn. Here, looking back, we got a good view of the bridge that spans the Sound between the Island of Seil and the Mainland. It is thirty feet high, to allow small coasting craft to sail underneath, and is said to have been the first instance in Britain in which an island was joined to the mainland by means of a bridge. On the right Loch Feochan and— nearing Kerrera—Gylen Castle, situated on a rocky promontory, come into view. Tradition says that this castle was built by the Danes, but it is now believed to be of somewhat later origin. A stronghold of the Macdougalls of Lorn, it was, during the civil wars beseiged and captured in 1647 by General Leslie. A considerable amount of historical interest attaches to Kerrera, from the fact of its being the place where Alexander II. died in 1249, when on his way to suppress a revolt of the Western Islanders; and a spot called Dalrigh, or the King's Field, is pointed out where his death occurred. We now enter the Sound of Kerrera, and on the right in a finely-wooded hollow, may be seen the castellated mansion-house of Gallanach (P. M'Dougall, Esq.). In a few minutes afterwards, on the right, we pass Kilbowie Lodge (A. Dunn Pattison, Esq.) and then come in sight of Altnacraig—picturesquely perched on a grey conglomerate cliff—the summer residence of Professor Blackie. The villa next to it is Dungallan House (Major Arnold). The hulk "Enterprise," moored in Ardentrive Bay, on the left, formed one of the Arctic Expedition, which in the year 1848, sailed under the command of Sir J. C. Ross in search of Sir John Franklin. Upon her second voyage, *via* Behrings Straits, under the late Sir Richard Collinson she passed three winters in the ice and virtually completed Franklin's North West Passage. She is now employed as the store ship for coals, &c., for the use of the Northern Lighthouse Commissioners' steamers Pharos, &c.

Dunollie Castle—the chief stronghold of the Lords of Lorn—one of the oldest and most picturesquely situated of our Western Highland ruins, is now seen to great advantage from the steamer, being thrown into bold relief against the sky-line. The ivy-clad donjon or keep is the principal part now remaining, but from traces which can still be distinguished of other buildings, we are led to infer, that originally the castle was of large proportions, and doubtless protected in the usual manner by outworks, moat, and drawbridge. The present lineal representative of the ancient Lords of Lorn, once so powerful as to defy and defeat the warrior king, Robert the Bruce, is Colonel C. A, Macdougall, whose mansion stands in a hollow behind the ruin. The Brooch of Lorn, snatched from the shoulder of the Bruce, in the combat near Tyndrum, is still preserved among the ancient relics of the family.

> "The Brooch of burning gold
> That clasped the chieftian's mantlefold,
> Wrought and chased with rare device,
> Studded fair with gems of price,
> On the varied tartans beaming
> As thro' night's pale rainbow gleaming."

Two years afterwards Bruce defeated Macdougall in the Pass of Brander. Upon the shore, about a quarter of a mile nearer Oban, is the huge conglomerate mass called *Clach-nan-con* or the Dog's Stone. Tradition says that Fingal used this rock as a stake to which he tethered his celebrated dog Bran; and those who believe this legend, can in proof thereof, point to the fact of the very considerable abrasion of the pillar at its base, just what might have resulted from its having been used in the manner asserted. Doubtless Bran like any other dog, occasionally broke his chain, and could some zealous antiquary only succeed in unearthing one link,—the "missing link,"—aye, even half a link of Bran's chain— surely, all doubt as to the authenticity of the legend would be for ever set at rest.

At Oban, those who desire to make the tours of Staffa and Iona, Loch Scavaig, Loch Coruisk, Skye, Gairloch, and Loch Maree, land. Also those who wish to proceed by *Morning Steamer* to Ballachulish (for Glencoe and Glenetive), Banavie and Inverness, while those *en route* for Inverness, who wish to avoid the early

start from Oban, remain on board, and go on to Ballachulish, Fort William, or Banavie, joining the Inverness steamer at these places on following morning. For information as to hours, &c., see Time Table page 16. Oban, not inaptly described as the Charing Cross of the Highlands, is a most convenient centre for making excursions in all directions. It is of comparatively modern origin, dating no further back than 1791, and its history has been uneventful. It originally belonged to Donald Campbell of Dunstaffnage, but since then there have been several changes of ownership. The principal proprietors now are, Robert Macfie, Esq., of Airds; A. W. Macdougall, Esq., of Soraba; and Colonel C. A. Macdougall, of Dunollie, who own respectively the southern, central, and northern portions of the town. Oban has made rapid progress within the last quarter of a century, as may be seen from the rental, which in 1847, was £1719; and is now (1886) over £20,000. There are a number of large and splendidly appointed hotels, capable of accommodating over 1,000 persons, a handsome Hydropathic Establishment in the Scottish Baronial style not yet completed, also numerous lodging-houses, and the hill sides are studded over with villas, most of which are let in the season. It has seven churches of various denominations, five banks, and two newspapers are published weekly. Occupying a position of great natural beauty, with a mild and healthy climate, and commanding views of scenery both extensive and grand, it is no wonder that Oban has become a favourite resort of the tourist. As Professor Blackie—our gay Grecian Gael—quaintly puts it,—

> " For Oban is a dainty place ;
> In distant or in nigh lands,
> No town delights the tourist race
> Like Oban in the Highlands."

We now bid adieu to the rapidly rising capital of the West Highlands, with its beautiful bay, and after "hugging" the Maiden Isle, and bestowing a parting glance on green mantled Dunollie, we enter Loch Linnhe. On our left we have the Island of Lismore (*Great Garden*), on the extremity of which is the lighthouse and beyond it the Sound of Mull, with Duart Castle frowning darkly from Duart Point, Mull, upon the high range of the Morvern Hills, opposite. On our right we have Loch Etive, with Dunstaffnage Castle crowning a wooded peninsula jutting out into the Loch; and in the background of mountains, Ben Cruachan, with his twin peaks almost in line, reigns king over all, monarch alike to Loch Etive and Loch Awe.

Dunstaffnage is supposed to have been of Pictish origin, and its history, like that of the earldom of Mar, is lost in the dim vista of antiquity. Here was for a long time preserved the famous Coronation Stone, the palladium of Scotland, originally brought from Ireland by Fergus, who deposited it first at Iona. It was taken by Kenneth II. about the year 850, from Dunstaffnage to Scone, and was subsequently removed by Edward I. to Westminster Abbey, where ever since it has formed the support of the chair in which the ceremony of crowning the monarchs of the British Empire is performed. An ancient monkish distich thus runs :—

> NI FALLAT FATUM, SCOTI, QUOCUNQUE LOCATUM,
> INVENIENT LAPIDEM, REGNARE TENENTUR IBIDEM,

and has been translated as follows by Sir Walter Scott:—

> "Unless the fates are faithless found,
> And prophet's voice be vain,
> Where'er this monument is found,
> The Scottish race shall reign."

"There were Scots," adds Sir Walter, "who hailed the accomplishment of this prophecy at the accession of James VI. to the crown of England." Kenneth M'Alpine having transferred the seat of government from Dunstaffnage to Forteviot, about 845, for some centuries thereafter Dunstaffnage is not noticed in the national annals, and only reappears when Robert the Bruce took possession of it after his victory over Macdougall of Lorn in the Pass of Brander. The castle and its domains were granted in 1436 to Campbell of Loch Awe. Two miles from Dunstaffnage further up Loch Etive, is the Cataract of Connel (Ossian's Falls of Lora.) The bed of the loch here contracts till it is barely two hundred yards broad, and being interrupted by an extensive ridge of sunken rocks, the tides, (which rise about 14 feet) rush with such tremendous force through the narrow channel that the roar of the waves may sometimes be heard several miles off. On the shore of Ardmucknish Bay, about a couple of miles from Connell, are the two remarkable eminences, *Dunmacsniochan*, and *Dun Bhail-an-righ* said to be the site of *Berigonium*, the Pictish capital of Scotland. Tradition has it that Fergus built a fortress here—at anyrate there are the remains of a vitrified fort. A few years ago it was examined by Dr. R. Angus Smith, who found some relics—notably part of a sword and an iron brooch—and the learned doctor says, —" No one who sees the arrangement of the vitrified wall will doubt that it has been done on a system."

At the foot of Cruachan, Loch Etive bends to the left for thirteen miles, till it approaches within five miles of Glencoe, and at the head stands big burly Buachaille Etive (2540 ft.) keeping ward at once o'er the Loch and the Glen, The tower now seen on the right is Loch Nell Observatory, and on the other side of the hill are the ruins of thrice burnt Loch Nell Castle (D. Campbell, Esq.) We now pass on the right the entrance to Loch Creran. The island of Eriska, (J. Meliss Stuart, Esq.) On Lismore, Tirefuar Castle, an ancient Scandinavian watch-tower may be observed. Soon we get a good view (right) of Airds House (R. Macfie, Esq.), situated at the head of the bay of same name, while higher up, amongst the trees, is Drimneil (Dr Laurie.) When abreast of the bluff—the western termination of Airds Bay—notice the strange rib of rock forming a natural arch, and which can best be likened to the fossilised leg of some gigantic, pre-Adamite mammoth.

We now reach Airds Pier, **Appin,** where there is a ferry to Lismore. Leaving Appin, we see on the left Sheep Island, on which are limestone quarries, and, on the right, Barriemore House, (Mrs Campbell). Stalker Castle, situated on a rocky islet, now comes in sight. This castle belonged to the once powerful family of the Stewarts of Appin, and was occupied by King James the Sixth, when on his hunting expeditions. The island in front is Shuna, with the ruins of Shuna Castle a little to our right, and on the mainland opposite, almost entirely

Appin

concealed by a thick wood, is Appin House, (Master Leny). Rounding Shuna we have on the left the mountains of Morvern, Kingairloch, and Ardgour, on the right the green hills of Appin—and straight ahead, we catch the first sight of brave old Ben Nevis—hoary and scarred by the ravages of time—but still towering proudly above all his fellows. Looking back down the Morvern coast, we may here get a glimpse of Castle-na-Churn, crowning a conical hill at the entrance to the glen of the same name. Forty minutes after leaving Appin we pass, on the right, Ardsheal House, (A. D. Anderson, Esq.), once one of the seats of the Stewarts of Appin. This family warmly espoused the cause of the Stuarts in the Rebellion of 1745, and their estates were confiscated, but were restored about 1770. A cave in Ardsheal hill is shown in which Colonel Charles Stewart hid after the battle of Culloden, until he was able to escape to France.

Ballachulish Pier — We are now entering Loch Leven, and in a few minutes arrive at Ballachulish Pier, where passengers land who intend to drive up Glencoe. As the steamer sweeps round after leaving the pier, we notice, charmingly situated in the wood at the foot of the glen on our right, Ballachulish Mansion House, (Lady de la Poer Beresford,) —the Beresford Arms Hotel on the wooded point,— North Ballachulish Hotel on the other side of the narrows, and further off, Aultnashellach House, (Rev. A. Chinnery Haldane, Bishop of Argyle.) Glencoe is now seen in the distance bending away towards the right, the entrance guarded by the conical hill called the Pap of Glencoe; while Loch Leven runs up for about eight miles through the glen on the left. Invercoe House, and the ruins of MacIan the chief's house, are in the wood close to the foot of the Pap. Between the head of Glencoe and the head of Loch Leven, is that bit of General Wade's military road yclept "The Devil's Staircase," and we fancy that to it applies the paradoxical couplet,—

"Had you seen this road before it was made,
You'd lift up your hands and bless General Wade."

The view here, looking either east or west, is at sunset —simply magnificent.

From Kirn on the Clyde till now all the land on our

right, and nearly all on the left has been Argyleshire, but Inverness-shire now comes in, and the district on the right is called Nether Lochaber. Nestling in a clump of trees near Onich Point, (on our right) we see Cuilchenna House, in which the late Rev. Dr. Norman Macleod resided for some years; and about a mile to the east of it, is the manse of Onich, Rev. Alexander Stewart, L L.D., a gentleman well known over the North and West Highlands by his literary *nom-de-plume* of "Nether Lochaber."

On looking in the direction of Glencoe, after rounding the Buoy off the Point, we can distinguish the upper workings of the celebrated Ballachulish Slate Quarries (lessee, Dr. Campbell), the largest in Scotland, and now wrought for nearly two hundred years. To the left, may be observed Ardgour House, and shortly, passing through the narrows, we enter Loch Aber, and arrive at Ardgour Pier. Fifteen minutes afterwards we come in sight (on the left) of Conaglen, the seat of the Earl of Morton, and close to the shore near here, is the rock on which Glengarry was killed in 1828, by rashly leaping overboard from the stranded steamer, "Stirling Castle." We have now, on the right, another view of Ben Nevis, while straight in front lies the Great Glen, through which the Caledonian Canal runs; and in a few minutes we arrive at Fort-William. (population about 2600.) The town has been at different periods of its history called Gordonsburgh, Duncansburgh, and Maryburgh. Of late years, its appearance has been very much improved by the new houses and villas that have sprung up in the outskirts, and it has several very good hotels. The Fort, situated at the east end, was originally built by General Monk in the time of Oliver Cromwell, to overawe the turbulent Highlanders, and was re-erected, but on a smaller scale, by William III. It withstood sieges during the rebellions of 1715 and 1745, and was garrisoned until 1864, when the Government sold it to Mrs. Cameron Campbell of Monzie, the superioress of the town. Leaving Fort-William we notice, on the right, the ruins of Inverlochy Castle, a large quadrangular structure, with massive round towers at each angle, the whole surrounded by a deep and wide fosse. Tradition says that it was at one time a royal palace, and that King Achaius here signed a treaty with Charlemagne. Inhabited afterwards by Banquo, Thane of Lochaber, it subsequently passed into the possession of the Comyns, whose ambition and turbulence caused their ruin. The plain near the Castle, was in 1646, the scene of a sanguinary conflict between the Marquis of Montrose and the Marquis of Argyll, and which is admirably described in the "Legend of Montrose." Argyll was defeated with a loss of 1500 men and had to seek safety on board his galleys, anchored in Camus-na-gael Bay on the opposite shore. Further off and higher up the plain is Torlundie or New Inverlochy Castle (Lord Abinger) where Her Majesty resided for some time in the autumn of 1873, and on her departure proceeded from Banavie to Inverness by the "GONDOLIER."

Neptune's staircase—a series of locks between Corpach and Banavie—is now visible, and after threading our way among the islands at the entrance of Loch Eil, which stretches for ten miles through the glen on our left, and passing an obelisk erected to the memory of Colonel John Cameron. K.T.S., who fell at Quatre Bras, at the head of the 92nd Highlanders, we arrive at Corpach. Omnibuses convey cabin passengers to Banavie (Lochiel Arms Hotel), and as all luggage which has been properly labelled is forwarded by vans to the hotel, passengers do not require to look after it. Banavie is a most convenient centre for making excursions to the following places, all of which are well worthy of a visit.—Prince Charles' Monument, Glenfinnan and Loch Sheil; Achnacarry, the seat of Donald Cameron, Esq., of Locheil, late M.P.; the parallel Roads of Glen Roy, Ben Nevis, and Glen Nevis where there are two fine waterfalls.

Corpach
Banavie.

BANAVIE TO INVERNESS,
(The Caledonian Canal.)

The distance from Loch-Aber on the west coast, to the Moray Firth on the east coast is 62 miles. The passage consists of 24 miles of canal and 38 miles of natural lakes; namely Loch Lochy (10 miles), Loch Oich (4 miles), and Loch Ness (24 miles). "The whole length of the canal, when extended on a map, measures only four miles longer than a straight line drawn from one extremity to the other." The canal was opened from sea to sea in 1822. The total cost of construction was a million of pounds sterling. The locks are each 160 feet long, and 38 feet wide, and the depth of water in the locks and reaches is from 17 to 18 feet. Vessels of between 600 and 1000 tons burden can pass through.

From Banavie, Ben Nevis, the monarch of all our British mountains, with the sun dispelling his morning crown of mist, looks glorious. Its height is 4406 feet above the level of the sea, 114 feet higher than Ben Macdhui, once reputed the highest in the united kingdom. It is 24 miles in circumference at the base, and is seen from here to very great advantage.

> Oh, for a sight of Ben-Nevis,
> Methinks I see him now,
> As the morning sun-light crimsons
> The snow-wreath on his brow,
> As he shakes away the shadows
> His heart the sunshine thrills,
> And he towers high and majestic
> Amid a thousand hills.

That this is no exaggeration of the poet, we shall be convinced as we view the countless shoulders and peaks of hills stretching away towards Glencoe and Morvern in the east, and Arisaig in the west—Locheil and Loch Linnhe giving a romantic aspect to the beautiful but stern surroundings. Fort-William is seen in the distance by the shores of Loch Aber, and nearer, on the banks of the river which gives it its name, is the grand old ruin, Inverlochy Castle. Near the suspension bridge over the Lochy is the Distillery from which comes the celebrated whisky called "Long John" or "Dew of Ben Nevis," and further on, at the foot of the great mountain at Torlundy, is Inverlochy House, the residence of Lord Abinger. There was great difficulty in making the part of the canal that lies between Banavie and Gairlochy, owing to the numerous rapid streams that flow from the west side into the Lochy. Sluices had to be made through the solid rock to convey these waters under the canal to the river, and the bed of the Lochy had to be raised twelve feet from its own natural bed to cause it to fall into the Spean at Mucomer.

Tor Castle is an old ruin standing on the west bank of the Lochy, not far from the Canal. It was at one time the residence of a chieftain of the clan Mackintosh, from whom the Camerons took it, as well as the lands around. Tradition points to this place as the spot chosen by Ailean-nan-Creach, or *Allan of the Forays*, to have recourse to the Oracle of the "*Tigh Gairm*," or "House of Invocation." He was one of the Locheils of the fifteenth century, who desired to extend the family estates by means fair or foul. This he did by taking the lands of his weaker neighbours by the power of the sword, and by stealing their cattle by creach or foray. There can be no doubt that Allan had, often in cold blood, committed many dark deeds, when lifting his neighbours' cattle. As years advanced the remembrance of those deeds came home to him, and conscience made him a coward. Remorse for the past, and dread of the future, rendered him miserable. In desperation he resolved to unveil the future, by extorting answers from the "spirits of evil." Having met them, his first and only question was, what acts ought he to perform to obtain pardon for his guilt? He was told he might obtain forgiveness for his many deeds of rapine and bloodshed by building seven churches throughout the country, one for each great foray. This he did, and the ruins of them are still to be seen at Kilmallie, Kilcoral (St. Cyril's), Kildonan, Kilchoan (in Knoydart), Arisaig, Morvern, and Laggan (in Badenoch). A little further on a dyke is seen on our left, running up the hill: this is the march that divides Argyleshire and Inverness-shire. Since passing Kirn till now we have been coasting Argyleshire; from this point to Muirtown is Inverness-shire. The house on our left is named Strone. A fine view can be obtained of Glenloy, with its beautiful river murmuring and wending its way, until its waters are discharged into the river Lochy. This lovely glen is luxuriantly clothed with trees, rising up from the banks of the river on both sides, and covering the hills. On the east side of the river, at the foot of the mountain, standing amid trees, is Erracht House, the birthplace of Lieutenant-General Sir Allan Cameron, K.C.B., a soldier who served with great distinction in the first American war, in Egypt, Sweden, Spain, and all through the Peninsular War, and who in 1793, raised in the short period of three months, the 79th Cameronian Highlanders, better known to some as the "Queen's Own." Near Gairlochy is the only place on this part of the route where the mountain-monarch, Ben Nevis, with its heights of everlasting snow, can be seen.

The first of the chain of lochs linked together by the Canal is Loch Lochy. It is ten miles long, with an average breadth of one mile. On our left is seen "Achnacarry Castle," the seat of Donald Cameron, Esq., of Lochiel, late M.P. for Inverness-shire. Near it are still standing the ivy-clad ruins of the old castle, which after the defeat of the Highlanders at Culloden Moor was burned by the Duke of Cumberland and his "red soldiers." For the part Lochiel took in the Rebellion of 1745 the estate was confiscated by the Crown, and its noble owner had, for many years, to seek an exile's home in France; but it was afterwards restored to him. It is encircled by hills, and is one of the loveliest and most romantic spots that can be seen. Near the house is the river Arkaig, a wild, romantic-looking stream, with wooded banks, dark pools, and a pretty islet near the mouth. Stretching away from the river towards the north is the "Dark Mile," a noble avenue where gigantic trees so weave and interweave their branches that, when covered with foliage, the sunshine cannot pierce it. About the middle of this avenue is a cave, which gave shelter to the unfortunate Prince Charlie in his flight from the field of Culloden. At the north end of the Dark Mile is Loch Arkaig, a beautiful loch running in northerly direction for about fourteen miles. It lies amongst the wildest and most romantic scenery, and along its shores, once resounding with the voices of strong men, and the mirth of children, there is now eternal silence, broken only by the cry of the sheep or red deer, the only denizens of that wide district. From its sides branch off many glens and "corries," the home of the eagle and red deer, and along its shores Prince Charles wended his solitary way to Skye, to effect his escape to France. On the west side of the loch is

Lochiel's Forest, where the Scotch firs wave luxuriantly, and the heather grows in some places to the height of six feet.

The late Arthur Hugh Clough visited this spot with a reading party from Oxford, and speaks of one of the glens in these words,—

> Yea, too, in Mealy Glen,
> The heart of Lochiel's fair forest,
> Where Scotch firs are darkest, and amplest, and intermingle,
> Grandly with rowan and ash !

On the east side of Loch Lochy, Glenfintaig House can be seen. Near it stands Glengloy House, recently built by the proprietor, George G. Mackay, Esq. It is flanked by high bare hills, with an ancient water beach, at an elevation of 1278 feet above the present sea level.

At right angles to Glengloy, and a few miles in an easterly direction, are the parallel roads of Glen Roy, forming a district of the greatest interest to the geologist. The existence of these roads was unknown to the scientific world till after the third volume of "Pennant's Tour in Scotland" had been published in 1776; and their remoteness may account for the fact that until the year 1817 no systematic description or scientific attempt at explanation of them appeared. In that year Dr. MacCulloch, who was then President of the Geological Society, presented to that Society a memoir in which the roads were described, and regarded as the margin of lakes once embosomed in Glen Roy. Subsequent examinations have suggested that the formation of these roads is due to the action of "Glaciers," as asserted by Professor Tyndall, Sir Thomas Dick-Lauder, Mr. Jamieson, and Agassiz. There are various conflicting theories, but the one generally accepted as the correct one is that given by Professor Tyndall.

At Kinloch-Lochy, in 1544, a fierce battle was fought between the Frazers and MacDonalds, which got the name of "Blàr na léine," or "The battle of the shirts," because, from the heat of the day, the combatants stripped to their shirts in this terrible melee, in which the Frazers were nearly all destroyed.

Laggan.

Laggan. about a mile from Kinloch-Lochy, adjoins

a cut in the canal. In Laggan is the burying place of the MacDonalds of that ilk.

Loch Oich commences three-quarters of a mile from Laggan, and is three-and-a-half miles long, and fully a furlong in mean breadth; and, having one-hundred feet of an elevation above sea level, forms the highest reach of the canal navigation. It has some pretty islets, and is surrounded by scenery which unites the majesty of Alpine grandeur with the softest sylvan beauty. Near the south-west extremity of Loch Oich is a strange old monument with an apex representing seven human heads, known by the name of "Tobar na'n ceann," or "The well of heads," and having the following inscription in four languages:—

> As a Memorial
> Of the ample and summary
> Vengeance
> Which, in the swift course of
> Feudal Justice,
> Inflicted by the orders of
> The Lord MacDonnell and Aross,
> Overtook the perpetrators of
> The foul Murder
> of
> The Keppoch Family,
> A branch of
> The Powerful and Illustrious
> Clan
> Of which His Lordship was
> The Chief,
> This Monument is erected by
> Colonel MacDonnell of Glengarry,
> XVII. Mac-mhic Alastair,
> His Successor and Representative,
> In the year of our Lord,
> 1812.
> The Heads of the Seven Murderers
> Were presented at the feet of
> The Noble Chief
> In Glengarry Castle,
> After having been washed
> In this Spring;
> And ever since that event,
> Which took place early in
> The Sixteenth Century,
> It has been known by
> The name of
> "Tobar-nan-ceann,"
> or
> "The Well of Heads."

The base deed of which this stone tells, may briefly thus be indicated:—Keppoch sent his two sons to France to be educated, and in their absence he died, leaving the management of the estate to seven kinsmen. On the return of the sons of the chief, their ruthless kinsmen murdered them, and took possession of their land. The bard of Keppoch went to urge Glengarry to vengeance, and this monument tells in graphic story the result of this terrible revenge.

Invergarry, beside the river, and at the mouth of the glen of that name, is in the middle of the west side of Loch Oich. The spot is the softest and loveliest on the route. The refreshing green of the hills and slopes, and the blending of wood and water, make up an exquisite picture. The scenery at Invergarry has often been compared to the most picturesque portions of the Rhine. A road passes through this glen to Tomdoun Inn, Glenquoich, and by Loch Hourn on to Glenelg, on the west coast. At Invergarry is the ruin of the old Castle, so long the home of the chiefs of the Macdonells of Glengarry, whose patronymic was "Mac-Mhic-Alastair," The rocky headland on which the ruin stands was called "Creagan nam Fitheach," which name became the slogan or war-cry of the clan, and woe betide the foe into whose ears the wild cry was sounded, down to dread Culloden's woeful day, when the "red soldiers" burnt the eyrie of this mountain eagle, and the spirits of the clansmen bold were broken. But though the Castle was burnt it was not wholly destroyed, for one flight of the stairs leading to the tower is still good. Near the old Castle is a fine new residence, built by the late proprietor, Edward Ellice. Esq., formerly M.P. for St. Andrews. At the north end of Loch Oich, near

Cullochy

Cullochy Lock, is Aberchalder, where Prince Charles Edward mustered his army before proceeding, belted and plaided, and in high spirits, to the lowlands.

About two miles from Cullochy is Kyltra Locks, where passengers can have a walk of two miles along the canal banks, and join the steamer again at Fort-

Fort-Augustus

Augustus. The old fort was built by General Wade, in 1729, to overawe the clans that had taken part in the rising of 1715, and accommodated about eight hundred officers and men. It has for years past been entirely useless, having been dismantled long ago, and is now the seat of the Benedictine Order in Scotland, and a noble and massive pile of buildings in the early

English gothic style now rears its walls where once
the Military Fort stood. Two grim bastions, the green
moat with its stone bridge, the officers guard-room,
the engine-house and military well are nearly all
that have been preserved as relics of the past. It was
shelled from the "Battery Rock" and taken after
two days by the Jacobite warriors on their southward
march, and afterwards re-occupied by the victorious army
of Culloden. Here a host of the Highland Lairds were
detained after the fatal battle of '46 ; here the bleeding
head of Robert Mackenzie was brought and delivered to
the Duke of Cumberland as that of Prince Charlie ;
here Lord Lovat was confined in a dungeon before being
taken to London for execution, whilst from its walls
issued the companies of savage soldiery who laid waste
and almost depopulated the neighbouring country.

In 1773 the Fort was visited by Dr. Johnson and
Boswell, then on their way to Skye. Four years
later, we find Dr. Johnson entering in his Diary that
he had passed the previous night in such sweet, uninterupted sleep as he had not known since he slept at
Fort-Augustus. The Fort was occupied till the
Crimean War, and then sold, in 1867, to the late Lord
Lovat for £5000, and in 1876 the present Peer made it
over together with sixteen acres of the surrounding land
to the Benedictine Order and the revenues of the adjoining farm of Borlam were added as an endowment for 19
years. Some idea of the scale on which the establishment has been constructed may be formed from
the statement that its cost is estimated at £80,000,
and its future church will not be less than £50,000.
The Institution comprises a quadrangle of four distinct
buildings — the College, Monastery, Hospice, and
Scriptorium—connected by exquisite cloisters in the
purest early English Gothic, and designed by P. P.
Pugin, of 111 Victoria Street, Westminster. These
cost some £8000. The Scriptorium is unique and
cost £1000. It is the monastic studio for painting,
illuminating and carrying on works of art. The Monks
have also established a printing press. The College is
connected with the Glasgow and London Universities
and its ordinary staff of Professors is supplemented by lay

University Professors, who live in a house apart from the College and, receiving their salaries from the Marquis of Bute, are known as the "Bute Professors." Tourists who wish to see this interesting establishment will be courteously received, and can obtain tickets of admission at the College gates for the sum of One Shilling. This fee goes to defray the cost of the clock and chimes (£800) from which the public derive so much convenience. As it takes the steamer about forty-five minutes to pass through the locks of Fort-Augustus, passengers will have ample time to visit the College and Cloisters and to ascend the great Tower. They also pass on the way John M'Donald's shop, noted for Highland crooks.

The Fort has a farther interest from being the place where Mrs. Grant of Laggan resided for some time with her husband, who was Chaplain of the Forces, and where she wrote her beautiful "Letters from the Mountains," composed the finest of her poems, mastered the Celtic language, and became an authority on Celtic matters. Her books on America are quoted by the Duke of Argyle as his highest authority, in his "First Impressions of the New World." About two miles from the Fort on our right, is Glendoe, one of the most sweetly rural, and, at the same time, wildly romantic spots to be met with anywhere. This glen is the birth-place of General Fraser, who passed his early years here, and was killed at *Saratoga*, in Burgoyne's expedition.

Loch Ness is twenty-four miles long. having an average breadth of a mile-and-a-half, though in some parts having only about half that width. The depth of this loch is very great—in some places 900 feet, which is the cause that it has never been known to freeze, a fact which of old gave rise to many superstitions on the subject. The sides of the hills on each side of the loch are luxuriantly clothed with oak, ash, birch, and fir, intermingled with a thick undergrowth of hazel, holly, and other varieties of copsewood. Who can forget the sight of all the sylvan beauty in this lovely place, where, in autumn, the glory of the purple heather, or, in early summer, the furze and broom, with their green and gold, and the fragments of red granite crags, gave a variety of colouring seldom seen; whilst the peculiar and beautiful sheen of the water of the loch imparts a rich tone to the whole, and fills up a picture of sweet enchantment, especially when the scene is lit up by the glory of the summer sky at sunset.

The first stage from Fort-Augustus, on the north shore, is **Invermorriston**, where an impetuous mountain stream flows into the lake. The river scenery, including the fall, is well worthy of a visit. Formerly the fall barred the ascent of salmon, but operations have been undertaken to enable the fish to run. The upper reaches of the river were a few years ago stocked with salmon fry, by the late Mr. Dunbar, of Brawl Castle. The old family mansion of the Grants of Glenmorriston looks out upon the lake. There is a beautiful drive through Glenmorriston on to Loch Duich and Lochalsh, in the Sound of Skye.

Invermorriston

A little further on, and on the opposite side of the loch, are the far-famed "**Falls of Foyers**." There is a pier here where passengers land, and where the steamer usually waits to give passengers time to visit the Falls. From the pier to the Falls there is a walk of about three-quarters of a mile by a winding path up a hillside which leads to where the greater Fall can be seen to the best advantage. The scenery all around is strikingly grand and picturesque. The smoke arising from the Falls looks in the distance as if from a furnace, hence the name given it in Gaelic, of "*Eas-na-Smùid*," which means the "Smoking Cataract." The river Foyers rises among the mountains of the "Monaliath," and runs thirteen miles along a high-based glen, overhung with wild mountains, and within a mile-and-a-half of its mouth makes two falls of respectively forty and ninety feet. Standing, awe-struck, gazing at the wondrous sight, the poet Burns wrote:—

"Falls of Foyers."

> "Among the heathy hills and ragged woods,
> The roaring Foyers pours his mossy floods,
> Till, full, he dashes on the rocky mounds,
> Where, through a shapeless breach, his stream resounds.
> As high in air the bursting torrents flow,
> As deep recoiling surges foam below,
> Prone down the rock the whitening sheet descends,
> And viewless Echo's ear, astonish'd, rends.
> Dim seen through rising mists and ceaseless showers,
> The hoary cavern, wide surrounding, lowers;
> Still through the gap the struggling river toils,
> And still, below, the horrid caldron boils."

All who are up the Canal should see this grand sight which the late Professor Wilson has declared "the most magnificent in Britain." On the opposite side of Loch Ness is "Mealfourvonie," a mountain of considerable height (2,400 feet), rising from a round base to a dome-like summit. Divach Burn, which empties itself into Loch Ness near Urquhart Castle, rushes down the northern side of the mountain, traverses a deep, romantic glen, and makes there an enormous leap, which, in times of heavy rain, may advantageously compare with the lower Fall of Foyers. On the side of this mountain there is a small tarn from which issues a stream called, "Ault Suidhe," or "The Resting Burn," which in the early years of the seventeenth century was connected with a terrible tragedy. There having been a feud between the Macdonnells of Glengarry and the Mackenzies of Ross-shire, a party of the Macdonnells of Glengarry crossed the hills to Beauly, and burned the Church of "Cill-a-Chriosd," in which was a congregation of Mackenzies. In the pursuit that followed, the leader of the Macdonnells sprang across a chasm of the "Ault Suidhe." An adventurous Mackenzie leaped after him, but fell short, and hung by the branch of a tree which he had grasped. Macdonnell turned, cut the branch with his knife, and the unfortunate Mackenzie dropped into the gulf, and was killed. The pibroch composed by Macdonnell's piper, while "Cill-a-Chriosd" was burning, is still known by the name of the church.

Inver-farigaig
Two miles further on the steamer touches at **Inverfarigaig** Pier, near to which is the pass of that name, an opening very little broader than the roadway which runs through it. It is one of the most romantic gorges in this part of Scotland. Both sides are covered with wood, except where the bald-headed Black Rock rises like a weather-beaten guardian of the pass. The summit of this rock was in ancient times the site of a vitrified fort, called Dun Jardil. A distinguished geologist, Dr James Bryce, of Edinburgh, was, in July, 1877, killed by a fall of rock while examining the strata in this pass. A memorial stone, pointing out the spot where the accident occurred, has since been erected by geological friends.

Further on, near Drumnadrochit, stands the hoary ruin of Urquhart Castle, besieged by Edward First when trying to subdue Scotland. It is a very fine ruin, and must have been a place of great strength, reminding one of the poet's words—"Time has made beautiful that which at first was only terrible." Glen Urquhart, which opens up above this castle, belongs to the Earl of Seafield, and in it is his own residence of Balmacaan.

Temple Pier, Urquhart

The beauties of Glen Urquhart have been often celebrated. The painter, Phillip, had a cottage here, situated near the fine falls of Dhivach. A comfortable and well-kept hotel at Drumnadrochit forms a favourite summer resort. On the occasion of a visit in the autumn of 1860, the late Shirley Brooks contributed a letter to *Punch*, which helped to make the spot famous. "The inn," he wrote, "whence these lines are dated, faces a scene which, happily, is not too often to be observed in this planet. I say happily, sir, because we are all perfectly well aware that this world is a Vale of Tears, in which it is our duty to mortify ourselves, and make everybody else as uncomfortable as possible. If there were many places like Drumnadrochit, persons would be in fearful danger of forgetting that they ought to be miserable." The inn has been often noticed in print, and always with commendation. The following verses are from an old "visitors' book":—

> Stop, Traveller! with well pack'd bag,
>   And hasten to unlock it;
> You'll ne'er regret it, tho' you lag
>   A day at Drumnadrochit.
>
> Stop, Angler! with your rod and creel,
>   If you with trout would stock it;
> I have nae doubt ye shall do weel
>   To stay at Drumnadrochit.
>
> Stop, Artist! with your sketching-book,
>   For gin ye can but tak' it,
> At Urquhart Castle ye should look—
>   'Tis close to Drumnadrochit.
>
> Stop, every one! who would combine,
>   Care both of health and pocket:
> You'll find short bills and breezes fine
>   Prevail at Drumnadrochit.

The Right Hon. John Bright writes as follows :—

"In Highland glens 'tis far too oft observed,
That man is chased away and game preserved;
Glen Urquhart is to me a lovelier glen—
Here, deer and grouse have not supplanted men."

Shirley Brooks, before quoted, and his friend, John Phillip, made frequent excursions from Drumnadrochit up through Glen Urquhart to Corrimony, and across the hill to Glenaffric, which is described as "a glen of the most exquisite beauty, and on the road may be seen every variety of Highland scenery, rich and wooded, wild and bleak, and a fierce, grim cataract (the Dog Falls), worth coming any distance to see."

This excursion is often extended to Strathglass, and tourists wishing to vary their route a little, and having time to spare, may find their way down past Struy, the Dreim, and Falls of Kilmorack, to Beauly Station, on the Highland Railway—10 miles distant from Inverness.

Four miles from Temple Pier the steamer passes *Abriachan*, where a pier has recently been erected. It is a pretty little spot, with a steep slope partially wooded, and a rural hamlet perched on a grassy eminence. The stream here has a picturesque channel, leaping down by a series of steps to find its repose in Loch Ness. A curious old burying ground lies close at hand—a grassy space in the midst of the copse, looking down upon the lake. In the centre is a rude square enclosure of stakes and branches, forming what seems a family burying-place. An interesting object may be observed just outside this enclosure ; two flat stones lie together, one quite plain, the other adorned with a decorated cross of very tasteful workmanship, belonging apparently to a pre-Reformation period. At the foot of the cross is the outline of a shears, probably of more recent date; and the supposition is that the stone has been brought from the tomb of some Templar in connection with old Urquhart Castle. Another interesting object is a stone with a round hole in the centre, which goes by the name of a baptismal font. According to legend, St. Columba from this font baptized the heathen Caledonians of the surrounding country. The font is said to be always filled with water, even in the driest weather. A Chapel is also said to have stood near the burying-ground.

On the north-eastern extremity of Loch Ness is Aldourie, in the old baronial style, the residence of Edward G. Fraser Tytler, Esq., a lovely spot, and a house that has nothing to jar on the eye that loves the beautiful. It was the birth-place of Sir James Mackintosh, the philosopher, statesman, and historian. On the opposite side, Dochfour House, a fine modern building in the Italian style, the seat of Evan Baillie, Esq., is next seen. A little further on is the source of the river Ness, and about half a mile beyond it, is Dochgarroch Lock. *Aldourie*

About three miles from Dochgarroch is Tomnahurich, a singularly shaped hill, rising from a level plain. Its summit is reached by a zig-zag road up through the trees that cover its sides, and on the top is the "City of the Dead," one of the most delightful places one could imagine for resting after "life's fitful fever" is over. The hill has a striking resemblance to a ship turned keel uppermost, and no visitor should miss seeing this old place, where it is said the prophet bard, Thomas of Ercildoune, is buried—indeed, tradition says the hill was piled over his remains—a tomb as eternal, and almost as great, as the pyramid built over the bones of Cheops. There are many legends about this hill, which is said to have been a favourite haunt of fairies, when fairies there were.

In a few minutes after passing Tomnahurich the steamer arrives at her destination. On a fine evening when the sun is going down, the view of Inverness and its surroundings from this point is lovely—the Castle on its elevated site looking quite picturesque, and the broad clear river winding its way to the sea; the hills in the background gay with purple heath and green ferns, look beautiful in the mellow light. In the distance the wooded braes of the "Black Isle" have a charming effect, whilst the Moray Firth shines like a sheet of silver all the way down to Fort George. Cabs and omnibuses from the different hotels await the steamer's arrival at Muirtown (the landing place for Inverness), and passengers will find plenty of good accommodation in the town. *Inverness*

Inverness, the capital of the Highlands, is a town with a population of about 18,000. It is an ancient burgh, having received in the twelfth century a charter from William the Lion. The situation is extremely interesting. The greater part of the town—the business part—occupies the flat on both sides of the river, but new streets and numerous villas stretch along the terrace, which rises above the valley. The Castle hill is the most accessible point from which a view can be obtained, and a very fine view it is, stretching from Mealfourvonie, at Loch Ness, to Ben Wyvis, in Ross-shire, and taking in, a diversified scene of hill and valley, river, firth, and woodland. The wooded hill which terminates the slope opposite the Castle hill is Craig Phadrick, well known to the antiquarian as having on its summit the remains of a vitrified fort, and where Hugh Miller made some of his earliest discoveries in Geology. In the town itself the visitor will observe the new Town Hall, recently erected at a cost of £12,000, and opened in January, 1882, by H.R.H. the Duke of Edinburgh. The building originated in a bequest of £5,000, left by a neighbouring proprietor, the late Mr. Grant, of Bught. In front of the Town Hall stands a very handsome Fountain, the gift of an old Invernessian (the late Dr. Forbes), and in its foundation is embedded the old "*Clach-na-cuddin* Stone," from which, in days gone by, all public proclamations were made. Union Street is generally admired for its regular and lofty buildings; and the railway station, with the hotel on one side, and suite of offices on the other, form a fine block. Four miles from Inverness is the battle field of Culloden, where the Stuart cause was finally crushed, in 1746. Professor Blackie says he has seen most of the fair cities of Europe, besides the finest in Africa, and one of the finest in Asia, and has always felt that, making allowance for its smaller proportions, Inverness may hold its ground against the best of them, and is in many of its most striking features superior to the great majority. "Such a happy combination of sea and land beauties, so much central culture with such an amplitude of wild environment, is very seldom to be found, not to mention the fresh breeziness, and comparative mildness and proved salubrity of the

climate." He has given to the world the following sonnet in praise of the northern capital:—

> Some sing of Rome and some of Florence; I
> Will sound thy Highland praise, fair Inverness:
> And, till some worthier bard thy thanks may buy,
> Hope for the greater, but not spurn the less.
> All things that make a city fair are thine,
> The rightful queen and sovereign of this land
> Of Bens and Glens and valiant men, who shine
> Brightest in Britain's glory-roll, and stand
> Best bulwarks of her bounds—wide-circling sweep
> Of rich green slope and brown-empurpled brae,
> And flowery mead, and far in-winding bay,
> Temple and tower are thine, and castled keep,
> And ample stream that round fair gardened isles
> Rolls its majestic current, wreathed in smiles.

The islands to which the Professor alludes in the above lines are a favourite resort in the summer evenings. They lie about three-quarters of a mile up the river, and are connected with each other and with the roadway on either bank, by means of suspension bridges.

From Inverness, two splendid short circular tours can be made by taking train to Strome Ferry, steamer (*via* Broadford, Plockton, and Raasay) to Portree and Gairloch, coach *via* Lochmaree, to Auchnasheen, and train to Inverness, or *vice versa*. (See pages 71, 72, 73 and 101); or by rail to Strome Ferry, steamer to Portree and Ullapool, coach to Garve, and train to Inverness, or *vice versa*. See pages 101, 102, 103, and 104.

OBAN to STAFFA and IONA and Back.

CABIN RETURN FARE, 15s.; Includes Guides and Boatmen.
Swift Steamer sails frequently in June ; and *daily* during July, August and September—

Going North.		Monday, Wed., & Friday. A.M.	Going South.		Tues., Thur., & Sat. A.M.
Oban	at	8 0	Oban	at	8 0
Craignure	about	8 35	Iona	about	11 30
Lochaline	,,	9 0	Staffa	,,	1 0p
Salen	,,	9 30	Tobermory	,,	3 15
Tobermory	,,	10 0	Salen	,,	4 0
Staffa	,,	12 0	Lochaline	,,	4 30
Iona	,,	2 5p	Craignure	,,	4 50
Oban	,,	5 30	Oban,	,,	5 30

A *Mail Steamer leaves Oban daily during the year (Sunday excepted) at* 12-45 *p.m., (after arrival of train, leaving Glasgow, Buchanan St., at* 7-10 *a.m.), for* **Tobermory.** *Returning from Tobermory daily at* 8 *a.m. for Oban (calling each way at Craignure, Lochaline, and Salen), in connection with* 12-40 *p.m. train for the South.*

Going by SOUND of MULL—Returning by South Coast of MULL.

This route is a sail round the Island of Mull; on Monday, Wednesday, and Friday the steamer goes by the Sound of Mull, and on the other days returns by it. On Wednesday evenings the steamer returns from Oban to Tobermory, thus enabling parties resident in Mull to visit Staffa and Iona and get home the same evening.

The boats for landing at Staffa and Iona are large, each capable of carrying from 30 to 40 passengers, and manned by the most experienced boatmen. A granite slip or pier for the landing of passengers has lately been built at Iona. At Staffa everything has been done for the comfort and safety of passengers, hand rails of wire-rope have been fixed from the entrance to nearly the end of Fingal's Cave, which enable passengers to go in without danger. A new stair, from the Clam-shell Cave, leads to the summit of the Island. The Steamer's fare includes boats, guides, and all charges, except meals on board.

Steaming out of Oban Bay, past Dunollie Castle, and through between the Maiden Island and the end of Kerrera, the steamer makes for Lismore Lighthouse, nearly opposite which, is the Lady Rock, completely covered at high water, and its position distinguished by an iron beacon. Tradition says that it was on this rock that one of the M'Leans of Duart placed his wife, expecting that the flowing tide would sweep her off She was rescued by one of her brothers, and the legend forms the subject of Campbell's spirited poem of "Glenara." On the first prominent point stands the old Castle of Duart. From this quarter is to be seen one of the finest pieces of scenery in Scotland. Looking backwards we see Ben Cruachan, towering above the Argyllshire hills; to the left Ben Nevis, the Peaks of Glencoe, with the waters of Loch Linnhe, Loch Creran, and Loch Etive; to the right the Island and Paps of Jura, and Colonsay; and, in front, the Kingairloch, Morvern, Ardnamurchan, and Mull hills.

We are now in the Sound of Mull, and after passing Duart Castle, we come in view of Torosay Castle, a splendid mansion, beautifully situated in Duart Bay, the property of A. C. Guthrie, Esq. The first place of call is **Craignure Ferry**, and at the head of Craignure Bay is Java Lodge (Misses Maclaine). The late Dr. Norman M'Leod resided here for some time. The steamer now crosses to the Morvern shore, where we see Ardtornish Castle, in which Sir Walter Scott has laid the opening scene of the "Lord of the Isles." Rounding Ardtornish Point the steamer touches at **Lochaline**, which is the landing place for the Morvern District. At the head of the Loch is the mansion of T. V. Smith, Esq., proprietor of Ardtornish. The next residence of note is Lochaline House, the property of the heirs of the late Mrs. Paterson; and further on the Manse of Fiunarie, a place immortalised to Highlanders as the early home of the late Dr. Norman M'Leod, the great Scottish divine, and editor of "Good Words." The late parish minister, the Rev. Dr. John M'Leod, was the uncle of Dr. Norman, and the second in succession of the same family that had filled this charge. Near Kilundine Point, close down at the water's edge, lies Con Castle. Kilundine House, the property of Col. Charles Cheape, stands higher up. The next place of call is **Salen Pier**, the landing place for this district of Mull, after leaving which we pass the fine old ruin of Aros Castle.

A magnificent view is now obtained of the saddle-shaped mountains, Ben Tallah and Ben More. The latter is the highest mountain in Mull, and is visible in varying shapes for most of the day. We are now in full view of **Tobermory**, or the Well of Mary, the bay of which forms a splendid anchorage for vessels of any tonnage, being protected by the Island of Calve, very much as Oban is by Kerrera. From the Pier, looking right across the bay, we see Drumfin Castle, the residence of Alexander Allan, Esq., of Aros. To the right of the Castle there is a very fine waterfall. The ship "Florida," one of the "Invincible Spanish Armada," is said to have been blown up, and to have sunk in the bay just below Drumfin.

<small>Tobermory.</small>

Steaming out of Tobermory, and looking towards the Morvern shore, is seen the chapel and residence of C. G. Gordon, Esq., of Drimnin; and here the Morvern hills terminate on meeting the waters of Loch Sunart, a very fine loch, which extends 17 miles inland. On the opposite side of the loch from Drimnin, on the Ardnamurchan shore, is Mingary Castle, a place of considerable importance in olden times, and still in splendid preservation. Passing Rhu na Gael Lighthouse, on the Mull shore, the first little bay is called Bloody Bay, from its having been the scene of a great sea fight some 400 years ago.

We are now on the waters of the Atlantic, and rounding Ardmore Point, we pass Glengorm Castle, the property of Wm. Lang, Esq. At Callioch Point looking in the direction of Arnamurchan Lighthouse we can see the Scuir of Eigg, the Island of Rum with its peaks, as also the Islands of Muck and Canna, the Cuchullin hills in Skye, and towards our left, Coll, Tiree, and the Treshnish Islands. Rounding Callioch Point, Calgary Bay and the Castle of Calgary, the property of J. Munro M'Kenzie, Esq., come in sight. At Treshnish Point, we get a view of Staffa, the Treshnish Islands, Fladda, the two Cairnburgs, Lunga, and Bach or the Dutchman's Cap, so named from the Island being shaped like the latter. One of these Islands, Cairnburg, has the remains of Danish fortifications still standing, though besiged at many different times. These islands are uninhabited, are all covered with very rich grass, and used for feeding a few Highland cattle. On the left hand Loch Tua opens up to view, with Torloisk,

the property of the Marquis of Northampton. Loch Tua is formed by the Mull shore and the Islands of Ulva and Gometra, and they again form another loch, called Loch-na-Keal, in the mouth of which lie the Islands of Inch Kenneth and Little Colonsay Loch-na-Keal nearly divides Mull, there being only four miles between its head and Salen pier in the Sound of Mull. The Channel Squadron anchored at the head of the loch in 1876. As we approach **Staffa**, we observe that the large red life-boat is waiting to land passengers. This boat comes daily across from the Island of Gometra (five miles off). The boatmen, before the steamer arrives, have decided upon the best landing place for the day, as it depends entirely on wind and weather which part of the island may be found most suitable. Sometimes the landing has to be made at the end of the island farthest from Fingal's Cave, at other times the passengers are landed right at the entrance, or are rowed into the cave in the small boat.

"This stupendous basaltic grotto in the lonely Isle of Staffa remained, singularly enough, unknown to the outer world until visited by Sir Joseph Banks in 1772. As the visitors' boat glides under its vast portal, the mighty octagonal columns of lava which form the sides of the cavern—the depth and strength of the tide which rolls its deep and heavy swell into the extremity of the vault unseen amid its vague uncertainty—the variety of tints formed by the white, crimson, and yellow stalactites which occupy the base of the broken pillars that form the roof, and intersect them with a rich and variegated chasing—the corresponding variety of tint below water, where the ocean rolls over a dark red or violet coloured rock, from which the basaltic columns rise—the tremendous noise of the swelling tide mingling with the deep-toned echoes of the vault that stretches far into the bowels of the isle—form a combination of effects without a parallel in the world! Staffa means 'the isle of columns.' In the isle are six great caverns. On proceeding from the landing-place the objects of interest that challenge our notice and excite our wonder are—first, the Clamshell Cave; second, the *Buachaille*, or Herdsman, third, the Causeway, and the Great Face, or Colonnade; fourth, Fingal's, or the Great Cave; fifth, the Boat Cave;

and sixth, the Cormorants', or MacKinnon's Cave, These columnar caves range, or vary, from 18 to 50 feet in height; the depth of dark water within them from 36 to 54 feet. The Great Cave, which is named from Ossian's King of Selma, is rather more deficient in symmetry than the rest. The outline of the entrance, perpendicular at the side, and terminating in a contracted arch, is pleasing and elegant. The height, says MacCulloch, from the apex of this arch to the top of the cliff above, is 30 feet; from the former to the surface of the water at mean-tide, 66 feet. The total length inward is 227 feet."

The following lines on Fingal's Cave are from the pen of Sir Walter Scott:—

> " The shores of Mull on the eastward lay,
> And Ulva dark, and Colonsay,
> And all the group of islets gay
>   That guard famed Staffa round
> Then all unknown its columns rose,
> Where dark and undisturb'd repose
>   The cormorant had found,
> And the shy seal had quiet home,
> And welter'd in that wondrous dome,
> Where, as to shame, the temples deck'd
> By skill of earthly architect,
> Nature herself, it seem'd, would raise
> A Minster to her Maker's praise!
> Not for a meaner use ascend
> Her columns, or her arches bend:
> Nor of a theme less solemn tells
> That mighty surge that ebbs and swells.
> And still, between each awful pause,
> From the high vault an answer draws,
> In varied tone prolong'd and high,
> That mocks the organ's melody.
> Nor doth its entrance front in vain
> To old IONA's holy fane.
> That Nature's voice might seem to say,
> " Well hast thou done, frail child of clay!
> Thy humble powers that stately shrine
> Task'd high and hard—but witness mine!"

Leaving the cave, we are conducted round the Causeway, where is pointed out the Corner Stone, being the only square stone on the island. From this point a very fine view is got of the Bending Pillars, seemingly bent out by the weight of the mass above them. Half way

along the Causeway is Fingal's wishing chair. Tradition says one has only to sit on it and wish three separate wishes, when they are all sure to be granted. We now ascend the stair to the top of the island, from whence we get the best view of the Clamshell Cave. This cave cannot be gone into either by boat or on foot. From the right hand side of the stair, looking down over the Causeway and the Herdsman, we have a wonderful view —pillars and stones in every conceivable shape, position and angle, and of every size, all seemingly built or fitted into each other. From the summit of the island M'Kinnon's Cave is to be seen, also Iona and its Cathedral Tower, and further off, Big Colonsay, Islay, and Jura, and to the left the Treshnish Islands, Coll, Tyree, &c.

On leaving Staffa the steamer keeps as close as possible to Fingal's, M'Kinnon's, and the Boat Caves, giving an opportunity of viewing them from the sea. After a sail of about 35 minutes the steamer reaches Iona, and upon being landed, passengers are conducted by the official Guide (appointed by the Duke of Argyll, who is the proprietor of the island), to the ruins of the Nunnery. Leaving these ruins we walk along what was called the Street of the Dead, past the Established Church and Manse, and "M'Lean's Cross." This cross is supposed to be the oldest in Scotland, being one of three hundred and sixty said to have been standing on the island, but of which only two now remain entire—it and another, "St. Martin's." The latter we shall see in the grounds of the Cathedral, as also the graves of the chiefs and the kings, of whom there are sixty said to be interred here; St. Oran's Chapel, with its fine Norman doorway and triple arch; and the Cathedral itself and St. Columba's tomb; the gravestones of Bishops, Abbots, and Monks, along with that of M'Leod of M'Leod.

Quite recently the Duke of Argyll has had some excavating done, displaying all the original foundations and plans of the buildings, and uncovering many splendidly carved stones that have lain for centuries, covered with rubbish.

Iona has a population of about 260, with two churches, Free and Established. The Free Church stands prominently on the point at Martyr's Bay, so called from the fact that it was at this place in olden times that the bodies of those who had suffered martyrdom were landed when brought to the island for interment. The Sound of Iona, separating Iona from the Ross of Mull, is here about a mile wide. The geological formation of the Ross is principally granite, and the quarries here supplied the red granite used in the construction of the Albert Memorial, Blackfriars Bridge, and the Holborn Viaduct. Lovers of nature and antiquarians could spend a few days profitably at Iona, visiting the Spouting Cave, Port-a-Churraich (the spot where St. Columba landed), the Cell of the Culdees; the Granite Quarries and the Lighthouse Station (for Dubh-heartach Lighthouse) on Earraid Island.

The run back to Oban is by the south of Mull and between the Torrin Rocks. The reef called the Torrins stretch to St. John's Rock, 16 miles off, upon which Dubh-heartach Lighthouse is built, and which can be easily seen in clear weather. Clearing these rocks and rounding Ardalanish Point, we get under the bold, high and precipitous headlands of Mull. The first, most prominent, and highest, rising almost perpendicularly from the sea, is called Gorry's Leap. Tradition says, that Maclaine of Lochbuy, having punished Gorry for some offence, the latter is said to have got his revenge in the following manner:—Maclaine with a party had been out shooting, when Gorry, by some means, got possession of the young Laird of Lochbuy, and rushing with him to the brink of the precipice, demanded that Maclaine should suffer the same indignity as he, Gorry, formerly had, otherwise he would jump over the precipice with the boy in his arms. Maclaine suffered the indignity before the eyes of Gorry and his own son; but even this did not appease the Highlander's appetite for revenge, for with one wild shout Gorry and the boy disappeared. We next come to the Carsaig Arches, the tallest standing up, guarding the point; they have a formation somewhat similar to Staffa. After passing the Arches we may get sight of a small opening in the side of the hill—the entrance to the Nun's Cave. The cave and its vicinity abound with valuable geological specimens and fossils of many kinds,

and from this neighbourhood is said to have been taken all the freestone originally used for building Iona Cathedral. The walls of the cave are said to be covered with carvings of crosses, &c., which are thought to be the original tracings of some of the Iona ones. We are now at Carsaig Bay, where the steamer usually calls. The Carsaig estate of Carsaig belongs to A. J. Maclean, Esq., of Pennycross.

We next reach Lochbuy, at the head of which can be seen the old and new castles of Lochbuy, standing side by side. The present proprietor is M. G. Maclaine, Esq. On Lochbuy Head we may have pointed out to us a small hole in the hill—almost imperceptible;—this is the entrance into a very large cave called Lord Lovat's, probably from an erroneous belief that that nobleman concealed himself in it for some time after the battle of Culloden.

Leaving Loch-Buy Head, the steamer now strikes off from the Mull coast, shaping its course for the Sound of Kerrera, returning to Oban by the opposite direction to which it left in the morning.

A Mail Steamer leaves Oban daily during the year (Sunday excepted) at 12-45 p.m., (after arrival of train, leaving Glasgow, Buchanan St., at 7-10 a.m.), for **Tobermory.** *Returning from Tobermory daily at 8 a.m. for Oban (calling each way at Craignure, Lochaline, and Salen), in connection with 12-40 p.m. train for the South.*

OBAN to MULL, SKYE, and GAIRLOCH.
Via Loch Scavaig, Loch Coruisk, and the Cuchullin Hills.

The Swift Steamer on this route (in addition to the Goods and Passenger Steamers), leaves Oban during July, August and September, every Tuesday, Thursday and Saturday, at 7 a.m.

	Tuesdays. a.m.	Thursdays and Saturdays. a.m.		Mondays, Wednesdays and Fridays. a.m.
Oban ....at	7 0	7 0	Gairloch.........at	6 30
Craignure....abt	7 45	7 45	Portree.. ......abt	8 30
Lochaline .... ,,	8 0	8 0	Broadford .... ,,	9 50
Salen........... ,,	8 30	8 30	Kyleakin ..... ,,	10 30
Tobermory... ,,	9 15	9 15	Balmacara ... ,,	10 45
Eigg............ ,,	10 30	10 30	Glenelg ...... ,,	11 0
Arisaig......... ,,	—	11 15	Isleornsay ... ,,	—
Loch Scavaig,arr	12 30p	—	Armadale .... ,,	12 0
Do. dep	1 30	—	Loch Scavaig arr	. —
Armadale ....abt	3 0	1 0p	Do. dep	—
Isleornsay.... ,,	—	—	Arisaig ..... abt	1 0
Glenelg ...... ,,	3 45	1 45	Eigg .... ,,	1 40
Balmacara ... ,,	4 5	2 5	Tobermory... ,,	3 15
Kyleakin .... ,,	4 25	2 25	Salen .... ,,	3 45
Broadford ... ,,	4 55	2 55	Lochaline..... ,,	4 30
Portree ...... ,,	6 0	4 0	Craignure ... ,,	4 50
Gairloch...... ,,	8 30	6 30	Oban ....arr	5 50

The times stated above are merely given for general information and are NOT guaranteed

Emerging from Oban Bay, which is crowded with yachts and steamers, we follow the same course across Loch Linnhe and through the Sound of Mull, as on the route to Staffa and Iona described on pages 55 and 56.

Leaving Tobermory, the entrance to Loch Sunart, is seen on our right, with Ben Shiand (1759 feet) on its western shore. Loch Sunart winds inland between the Morvern hills for about twenty miles. Near the scattered village of Kilchoan, are the ruins of Mingary Castle, in bygone days the seat of the MacIans, a branch of the Clan MacDonald. Away across the isthmus of Ardnamurchan we get a transient view of the pyramidal mountains of Rum ; and in the far north, the Cuchullin hills, "like sleeping kings," towering in lofty grandeur high above all.

On the left we pass Rhu-na-Gael Lighthouse (55 feet), and a little further on, Bloody Bay, where a sanguinary battle was fought between Haco of Norway and the MacLeods of Skye. Conspicuous on the heights above is Glengorm Castle, the residence of William Lang, Esq. Leaving the Sound of Mull we round the point of Ardnamurchan the westernmost extremity of the mainland of Scotland; and now the islands of Muck, Eigg, Rum, Canna, and Skye come fully into view, with Ardnamurchan Lighthouse (180 ft.) on our right.

The island of Muck belongs to Captain Swinburne. The inhabitants numbered 140 in 1773, but they all emigrated to America in 1828. Now, except a couple of herdsmen, the island is unoccupied by human being.

The island of Eigg (18 miles in circumference), the property of Professor Macpherson of Edinburgh, has about 250 inhabitants, principally small farmers and fishermen. The Scuir of Eigg, a basaltic column with the ruins of a fort on the top is described by Hugh Miller as "a tower three hundred feet in breadth, by four hundred and seventy feet in height, perched on the apex of a pyramid like a statue on a pedestal." A good hotel has been established on the island.

The Cave of Francis (Uamh Fhraing), near the shore was the scene of a tragedy almost unequalled in the annals of Celtic history, and which perhaps we had better here relate. About 230 years ago, the MacLeods of Skye, thirsting for vengeance on the Eiggites for a supposed injury, set sail for the island. The inhabitants (who numbered 200 at that time) suspecting the MacLeods' malevolent intent, repaired in a body to the cave —which is nearly invisible from the outside, but large and roomy within, being 260 feet long, 27 feet broad, and 20 feet high. The MacLeods plundered and burned the deserted huts, and were preparing to leave after a fruitless search for the inhabitants, when they happened to observe one of them, who had been sent out to reconnoitre. Quickly disembarking they reached the vicinity of the cave, and a slight fall of snow having occurred, they traced his footprints to the entrance. With diabolical ingenuity they gathered all the combustibles in the immediate neighbourhood and set fire to the immense pile. Prayers for mercy softened not their obdurate hearts; curses and imprecations were of no avail. And thus, in those lawless times, was the island of Eigg depopulated. Sir Walter Scott describes the tragedy in the following lines:—

> "The chief, relentless in his wrath,
> With blazing heath blockades the path;
> In dense and stifling volumes rolled,
> The vapour fill'd the cavern'd hold!
> The warrior threat, the infant's plain,
> The mother's screams, were heard in vain!
> The vengeful chief maintains his fires,
> Till in the vault a tribe expires!
> The bones which strew that cavern's gloom,
> Too well attest their dismal doom."

Both Muck and Eigg contain monastic remains, which, it is alleged, were raised by Saint Columba about the beginning of the seventh century.

The district of Moidart, to the north of Ardnamurchan, possesses a peculiar interest, being the landing-place of "Bonnie Prince Charlie" on the 25th of July, 1745, and from this place he sailed, after leaving "the field of the dead" (Culloden), on the 20th September, 1746.

On the southern shore of Loch Moidart stand the ruins of Castle Tyrim, once the seat of the Clan Ranald. In 1715, when the brave old chief of the clan set out to join the Earl of Mar in the campaign which ended on Sheriffmuir, he burned his ancestral home rather than leave it unprotected; and thus effectually prevented his enemies, the Campbells, from taking possession.

On the way to Loch Scavaig, where the steamer calls every Tuesday, we enter the sound between Muck, Rum, and Eigg.

The island of Rum is thirty miles in circumference, and is the property of Farquhar Campbell, Esq., whose house we observe at the head of Loch Scresor. Bloodstone was once quarried at the south-west corner, but being of inferior quality, the work was discontinued. The three highest peaks are—Haskeval, 2667 feet; Haleval, 2367 feet; and, at the south-east corner, Scuir-na-gillean, "The young lad's hill," 2504 feet.

The inhabitants, numbering 150, are descendants of a few families who came over from Skye in 1828, when the original inhabitants joined those of Muck and Eigg, and emigrated to America.

The Island of Canna lies to the north-west of Rum, and is 18 miles in circumference. Compass Hill, on the north-east end, contains so much magnetic iron ore, as to affect the compasses of passing vessels. Near the entrance to the harbour are the ruins of an old castle, where, tradition says, one of the Lords of the Isles imprisoned a Spanish lady, and the inhabitants assert that, at "the witching hour of night, when churchyards yawn, and graves give up their dead," her wraith is visible, hovering around the antiquated ruin.

Sir Walter Scott, in referring to the story, describes in the following lines how the lady whiled the weary hours away—

> " . . . . when moon on ocean slept.
> That lovely lady sat and wept
> Upon the castle wall ;
> And turn'd her eye to southern climes,
> And thought, perchance, of happier times—
> And touch'd her lute by fits, and sung
> Wild ditties in her native tongue.
> And still, when on the cliff and bay,
> Placid and pale the moonbeams play,
> And every breeze is mute—
> Upon the lone Hebridean ear
> Steals a strange pleasure mix'd with fear ;
> While from that cliff he seems to hear
> The murmur of a lute ;
> And sounds as of a captive lone,
> That mourns her woes in tongue unknown."

As we approach **Loch Scavaig**, the Cuchullin hills attract our attention. To the left may be seen the little island of Soa; the lonely home of a few fishermen. We steam in near the head of the loch, and, after anchoring, are rowed ashore in large and comfortable boats. A few minutes' walk brings us with beating hearts in full view of Loch Coruisk—the solitude only intensified by the plaintive sough of the wind and the ceaseless gurgle of the mountain torrents. Wilson truthfully paints Coruisk

[margin: Loch Scavaig]

in the following graphic and highly interesting sketch: "The dead, dull lake lay beneath; the ruins, as it were, of a former world were scattered on all sides; and above, as far as the eye can pierce through the murky clouds, rose the vast rocky pinnacles, their extremest heights obscured except at intervals, when we could behold the grim and awful giants keeping their eternal watches. The sides of these mountains, from the almost constant atmospheric moisture, are dark and damp, but there are thousands of small silvery streaks of waterfalls coursing downwards, which occasionally catch the gleaming lights, and throw a partial cheerfulness over the prevailing sadness of the scene. There was nothing within the visible diurnal sphere that breathed the breath of life—no sound, nor sight of any moving thing—nothing but a dead and stony, seemingly a God-forsaken, world. We almost longed, in this cloud-capped, thunder-stricken region. to hear the voice of gladsome bird, or even of murmuring bee,—but all, so far as regarded living nature, was silent as the grave. Only once we heard the resounding voice of some far avalanche of rocks and stones, sent rolling down the great breast of the opposing mountain. Just as we had risen to descend the rocks, there was a great break in the heavens above, a flood of far-flashing light was thrown upon the vast o'erhanging mountains, and into the gloomy gorges by which they were divided, and for a few minutes we could see glittering waterfalls and giant-peaks above the wreathed clouds, and small, pure breathing places, through the deep, blue sky. This splendour, however, was but of brief duration. Vast streams of misty vapour rolled into the hollows of the upper mountains, and obscured each peak and pinnacle which overhung the deep ravine. The whole scene from first to last exceeded in its sterile grandeur whatever we had previously seen in this, perhaps in any other country."

Sir Walter Scott appreciated Loch Coruisk's sublimity, and immortalizes it in the following exquisite lines :—

"Yes! 'twas sublime, but sad—The loneliness
Loaded thy heart, the desert tired thine eye;
And strange and awful fears began to press
Thy bosom with a stern solemnity.

> Then hast thou wish'd some woodman's cottage nigh,
> Something that show'd of life, though low and mean;
> Glad sight, its curling wreath of smoke to spy;
> Glad sound, its cock's blythe carol would have been,
> Or children whooping wild beneath the willows green.
>
> Such are the scenes, where savage grandeur wakes
> An awful thrill that softens into sighs;
> Such feelings rouse them by dim Rannoch's lakes,
> In dark Glencoe such gloomy raptures rise;
> Or, farther, where, beneath the northern skies,
> Chides wild Loch-Eribol his caverns hoar—
> But, be the minstrel judge, they yield the prize
> Of desert dignity to that dread shore,
> That sees grim Coolin rise, and hears Coriskin roar."

Retracing our steps, we reach the boats, and in a few minutes are again on board the steamer, which starts immediately on our arrival. Rounding the point of Sleat, we pass on the left Tormore House (D. Macdonald, Esq.) As we enter Armadale Bay, Lord MacDonald's *Armadale* Castle is conspicuous, surrounded by luxuriant trees. Further on we see the Established Church and Manse (parsonage), and on a promontory near the shore, the ivy-covered ruins of Knock Castle.

Loch Nevis ("loch of heaven"), on the opposite side, divides the districts of Morar and Knoydart. Isleornsay *Isleornsay* light is passed on the left, and, as we round into the bay, the little village of Isleornsay appears. Duisdale House (Miss MacKinnon) is pleasantly situated on the craggy shore. On the right we observe the entrance to Loch Hourn, which, by the way, signifies the "lower regions," so termed, we may safely infer, from its wild and gloomy appearance. The precipitous peak of Ben Screel, on its northern shore, is 3196 feet high. Crossing the Sound of Sleat, we reach Glenelg. From this *Glenelg* a road crosses by the head of Loch Duich to Invergarry, on the Caledonian Canal, and affords many striking and picturesque views to the pedestrian tourist. The ruins of the Bernara Barracks are seen at a little distance from the inn. They were built and garrisoned, after the rebellion of '45, to keep the Highlanders in check.

Sweeping round the head of the Sound, we pass through a narrow channel called the Kyle-Rhea, and emerge into Loch Alsh. The wall which we observe on the right, is the boundary line between the shires of Ross and Inverness. An old story says the rocky islet on our left, called Clach-Chuir, or the "putting stone," was thrown after an escaping prisoner by an irate giant, who for many years infested the district.

Loch Duich, a very beautiful and picturesque loch, winds among the hills to the right. On an island at the entrance to this loch are the ruins of Eilan Donan Castle, the ancient stronghold of the MacKenzies of Kintail. It was partially destroyed by an English war ship in 1719, and has since remained unoccupied.

Balmacara **Balmacara** Hotel and Balmacara House (Misses Lillingstone) are conspicuous on the right. (It may be as well to state that the tract of country on the right is generally called Lochalsh, so that the tourist may not confuse it with the loch of the same name on which we are now sailing). A monument has been erected on an eminence near the shore by Sir Roderick Murchison, the geologist, to commemorate the faithfulness, fearlessness, and integrity of his ancestor, Donald Murchison, factor for the Earl of Seaforth—Mackenzie of Kintail—during the stormy time of the rebellion of 1745. He collected the rents, for ten years, on the Seaforth estates—which were then confiscated—in defiance of the English, and transmitted the money to Spain, where the Earl had taken refuge. On the Earl's return, however, his services were ill requited; he was treated with coldness and neglect, which his haughty spirit could not brook, and he died of a broken heart, in the prime of life, at his native home in the wilds of Strathconon.

On the left stands the ruins of Castle Moil, built by a Danish Princess called "Saucy Mary," who stretched a chain across the Sound, and allowed no vessel to pass Kyleakin without paying her toll. The village of **Kyleakin** is a pleasant resting place for the tourist, and especially to the artist, possessing as it does some of the finest landscapes in the Western Highlands. Ben-na-Cailleach ("the old woman's hill") rises 2387 feet, behind the village. We pass Kyleakin lighthouse (60 ft.) on the right, and Loch Carron, stretching among the hills behind us, with Strome Ferry Station, the terminus of the Dingwall and Skye section of the Highland Railway, on its southern shore. The little island of Pabba on our right, is of remarkable interest to the geologist.

We now touch at Broadford where tourists sometimes land to visit the Cuchullin Hills, Loch Scavaig, and Coruisk, Ben-na-Cailleach, one of the "Red Coolins" (2385 ft.), is conspicuous, before and after leaving Broadford.

"To list his notes, the eagle proud
Will poise him on Ben-Cailleach's cloud."

The island of Scalpa, on our left, contains the ruins of the ancient chapel of St. Fillan a contemporary of St. Columba. Passing through the Kyle Mhor, between the islands of Raasay and Scalpa, we enter the Sound of Raasay. On the shore of the latter island, are seen the ruins of numerous huts, with green patches of land attached to each. The inhabitants were in the habit of literally tethering their children to neighbouring trees, to prevent them from falling over the cliffs into the sea; hence the place is called "Baille-nan-gibean," or "the town of the tethers."

Raasay belonged originally to the Macleods. The ruins of their ancient fortress (Brochel Castle) stands on a precipitous rock, overlooking the sea, on its eastern shore. On the top of Duncane (1443 ft.)—where they could view the various scenes of their labours—the Macleods are said to have annually treated their tenantry to a feast when their harvest was over.

Of late years this island has passed through many hands. It has been greatly improved by the present proprietor (Herbert Wood, Esq.), whose mansion we observe in a sheltered retreat overlooking the Sound.

The entrance to Loch Sligachan is seen on the left, with Ben Lea (1473 ft.) on its northern shore, and surmounted on the opposite side by the huge block of Ben Glamaig, 2670 feet high. Near the water's edge is the shooting lodge of Sconscer.

As we round into Portree Harbour, the hills rising almost perpendicularly from the sea, are at their base honeycombed by the action of the water into numberless caves. Ben Inivaig (1346 ft.) crowns the heights on our left. On the right, the outline of the hill takes the shape of a huge ram, somewhat resembling the bows of our ironclads.

Portree ("the King's Port") so called from having been visited by James V. of Scotland, while cruising round the western isles, appears, from the steamer, quite a picturesque little place. Here tourists land to visit the Quiraing—basaltic pillars at the north end of Skye—21 miles distant; and here is the best starting-point for the Cuchullin Hills and Loch Coruisk, by way of Sligachan, 9½ miles distant. Excursions are made in small boats to Prince Charlie's Cave, four miles from Portree, and also to the Storr Rocks.

Portree contains 2500 inhabitants, principally engaged in fishing and cloth weaving; and observes MacCulloch: "If there be any doubt in your mind respecting the progress of civilisation in the islands, come to Portree—it possesses a jail." Portree, however, has advanced with rapid strides since visited by MacCulloch. It has now four hotels, a post and telegraph office, and branches of three Scotch banks. A fine view of the Storr Rocks and the tops of the Cuchullins is got from the ruins of a small tower on a wooded eminence above the pier.

Leaving Portree for Gairloch, Loch Maree, and Inverness, we re-enter the Sound of Raasay. The entrance to Prince Charlie's Cave is discernible near the shore on the left, before passing the little island of Holm. This cave is the scene of Thomas Duncan's famous picture, representing the Prince asleep in the inner cavern, with the faithful Flora Macdonald guarding the entrance.

Above the island of Holm are the Storr Rocks, with the "Old Man of Storr"—a pinnacle 160 feet high—conspicuous in the front Further on, is the Kilt Rock, so called, from the perpendicular, basaltic pillars, chequered by horizontal strata, resembling "the garb of old Gaul." After a heavy rainfall a fine cascade of 300 feet dashes over the cliffs to the north of the Kilt Rock.

On the right, we pass the rocky island of Rona, separated from Raasay by a narrow channel. At one time, the sole occupants of this island were a fisherman, his wife, and three sons. The father and sons, while returning from the Minch, on a dark and stormy night, mistook their course, and were wrecked on the sunken rocks to the north of the island. The poor woman, thus suddenly bereaved, kept a candle burning in her window every dark night afterwards, until her praiseworthy efforts were rewarded, by being appointed lighthouse keeper in the handsome and substantial edifice at the north end of the island, erected principally through her instigation.

Emerging from the Sound of Raasay, we enter the Minch. On the left is seen the northern part of Skye and some of the Hebridean Islands, in the distance. On the right are the Torridon Hills; and behind we have a beautiful panorama of the mountains of Skye, with, it may be, the golden glory of the setting sun around their majestic heads. How many of us now may say with the old Highland bard on leaving his native Skye:—

"Farewell to each cliff, on which breakers are foaming;
Farewell each dark glen, in which red deer are roaming;
Farewell lovely Skye—to lake, mountain, and river—
Return—return—return we shall never!
(*Cha till, cha till, cha till sinn tuille !*")

As we approach **Gairloch** (two hours' sail from Portree), the low-lying lands on each side of the loch are not very attractive. In a little creek on the right, is the village of Badachro, formerly an important fishing station. Rounding into a sheltered corner of the bay the pier is reached, and we leave the steamer. Carriages are in waiting to take us to the hotel; and after starting, we pass on the right Flowerdale House, snugly ensconced amid an exuberancy of large and beautiful trees, the residence of Sir Kenneth MacKenzie, Bart., the proprietor of Gairloch. The Established and Free Churches are passed on our way to the hotel, which is a comfortable building, with superior accommodation, commanding a very fine sea prospect. Near the sandy shore, a little distance off, are the remains of a vitrified fort.

From the hills above Poolewe, six miles from Gairloch, a magnificent view of Loch Maree, studded with its seven-and-twenty islands, is obtained. The following lines descriptive of Loch Maree are from the pen of the Rev. Mr. Small :—

"In rugged grandeur by the placid lake,
Rise the bold mountain cliffs, sublimely rude,
A pleasing contrast, each with each, they make
And, when in such harmonious union viewed,

Each with more powerful charms appears imbued.
Even thus it is, methinks, with mingling hearts ;
Though different far in nature and in mood ;
A blessed influence each to each imparts,
Which softens and subdues, yet weakens not, nor thwarts."

We may return by steamer every Monday, Wednesday, and Friday morning, or leaving Gairloch by coach, a six mile drive, through moorland scenery, diversified by thriving plantations and pleasing waterfalls, brings us in sight of Loch Maree. Passing on by the side of the loch, the "Victoria Falls" are seen near the road on the right. As we emerge from the wood—Talladale Hotel, where Queen Victoria resided for a week in 1877, is passed on the left. A monument has been erected in proximity to the road, to commemorate the royal visit. After passing the hotel, we get a glimpse of the famous Isle Maree—a little wooded islet near the opposite side of the loch. This island, which contains the ruins of a monastery, was in days of yore the oasis of learning in the desert of heathenism. The waters of a little well that was on the island were said to have been effectual in curing mild cases of insanity. Whittier, in his poem on Loch Maree, refers to the well in the following lines :—

"Calm on the breast of Isle Maree
  A little well reposes:
A shadow woven of the oak,
  And willow o'er it closes.
And whoso bathes therein his brow,
  With care or madness burning,
Feels once again his healthful thought,
  And sense of peace returning.
Life's changes vex, its discords stun,
  Its glaring sunshine blindeth ;
And blest is he who on his way
  That fount of healing findeth !"

A Danish Prince appointed the island as the meeting place for his *fiancée*, the daughter of an Irish King. Having heard that the vessel was observed approaching Poolewe, he sent his messenger thither to ascertain if the lady had come. They were preparing to hoist a white flag—the agreed upon signal—to announce her arrival, when she, wishing to test his affection, ordered a black flag to be unfurled instead, upon seeing which, the prince,

FLOWERDALE, GAIRLOCH, ROSS-SHIRE.

whose mind was overcome with anxiety, put an end to his existence. The sad result being conveyed to her, she died in a paroxysm of despair; and the two flat stones, lying side by side within the monastery ruins, mark the grave of the unfortunate lovers. Though fate's stern fiat parted them in life—in death they are not divided:—

> " Far let me wander down thy craggy shore,
>   With rocks and trees bestrewn, dark Loch Maree;
> Till that green isle I view, whence, gazing o'er
>   Thy placid flood, long looked the prince to see.
> If yet the expected signal told that she,
>   His own loved princess, his betrothed bride,
> Drew near, his own for evermore to be;
> Then, when the black flag he afar descried,
> In heedless sport displayed, sank shuddering down and died."

Rising to the height of 4000 feet, at the south end of Loch Maree, is the imposing mountain of Ben Slioch. Passing the inn at Kinlochewe, we reach Auchnasheen, 28 miles from Gairloch, where we leave the coach, join a branch of the Highland Railway, and proceed by Dingwall and Beauly to Inverness, and return either by swift steamer, *via* Caledonian Canal, to Oban or Glasgow, by Highland Railway, *via* Dunkeld, Killiecrankie, &c., or by Great North of Scotland Railway, *via* Aberdeen.

OBAN to BALLACHULISH (Glencoe), FORT-WILLIAM, CORPACH, and back to OBAN.

STEAMER LEAVES	Daily July Aug. & Sep. A.M.	Daily Duri'g Seas'n P.M.	*Duri'g Seas'n P.M.	STEAMER LEAVES	†Duri'g Seas'n A.M.	July Aug. &Sep. A.M.	*Duri'g Seas'n A.M.
Oban ....at	6 0	12 45	4 50	Inverness...... at	..	..	7 0
Appin............,,	6 40	1 30	5 25	Banavie ....,,	4 45	8 45	3 35P
Ballachulish ....,,	7 30	2 30	6 15	Corpach ... .,,	5 5	9 0	3 50
Corpach......,,	7 55	2 50	6 40	Fort-William ...,,	5 15	9 20	4 0
Fort-William ..,,	8 30	3 30	7 15	Corran ....,,	5 45	10 0	4 35
Corpach......,,	9 0	3 50	7 30	Ballachulish ....,,	6 5	10 20	4 55
Banavie.........,,	9 20	4 0	7 50	Appin ....,,	7 0	11 20	6 0
Inverness ......,,	6 30p	..	..	Oban ....,,	7 40	12 15P	6 45

* In May, June, and October, on Monday, Wednesday, and Friday only.
† In May, June, and October, on Tuesday, Thursday, and Saturday only.

The above information is given for the convenience of Passengers, but the Proprietor reserves the right of altering these arrangements at any time he may find it necessary, and does not guarantee the times stated above.

In July, August, and September, the swift steamer leaves Oban daily at 6 A.M., and conveys passengers same day to Inverness.

The Mail Steamer leaves Oban daily during the year (Sunday excepted) about 12-45 p.m., (after arrival of train, leaving Glasgow, Buchanan St., at 7-10 a.m.), for **Fort-William.** *Returning from Fort-William every morning for Oban (calling each way at Lismore, Appin, Ballachulish, and Corran), in connection with 12-40 p.m. train for the South.*

Passengers leaving by the morning steamer from Oban, in July, August, and September, can proceed to Fort-William and Corpach and back to Ballachulish, drive through Glencoe and back and return to Oban same evening. The mid-day steamer from Oban (12-45) is the most suitable to go with for Glencoe. Time is giving at Ballachulish to drive through the glen and back; coach fare, 5/6. Also from Oban at 4-45 p.m., returning following morning.

A description of this route is given in pages 32 to 36. The drive through Glencoe is very grand.

Passengers not going direct to Inverness, but who wish to see Glencoe, can leave Oban in July, August, and September, daily at 6 a.m. or 12-45 p.m. for Ballachulish, and proceed from there at 2-30 p.m. or 6-15 p.m. for Fort-William or Banavie, or remain over night at Ballachulish; leaving following morning at 7-30, and arriving in Inverness same evening.

From Fort-William or Banavie the ascent of Ben Nevis can easily be made;

NEW ROUTE FOR TOURISTS.
GLASGOW AND THURSO.
In connection with the Railways at Oban, (Strome Ferry,) and Thurso.

DURING SUMMER
SPECIAL TRIPS WILL BE MADE BY THE SPLENDID STEAMSHIP
"CLAYMORE," or "CLANSMAN,"

Leaving Glasgow on dates advertised, at 12 noon (Train, Central Station, to Greenock, 4 p.m.) calling at Oban, Tobermory, Portree, Stornoway, Lochinver, Thurso, and numerous intermediate ports.

CABIN FARE, GLASGOW TO THURSO, *35s*; RETURN *55s.*

On advertised dates passengers may proceed by Columba via Crinan to Oban, and there join the Claymore or Clansman, following morning.

The route taken by the steamer as far as Stornoway is similar to that described on pages 91 to 100, and one of the most interesting places beyond on the way to Thurso is

THE ISLAND OF HANDA,

From "Notes on Handa and its Bird Life;" by James Lumsden, Esq., of Arden, Dunbartonshire. From the Proceedings of the Stirling Natural History and Archæological Society. 1885.

To observers of bird life and rock scenery the Island of Handa, one of the largest breeding places of sea birds on the coast of Scotland, is well worth a visit. The name Handa is Gaelic, either *Aon-dath*—one colour, or *Aon-taobh*—one side. It lies on the west coast of SUTHERLAND, 4 miles from the village of SCOURIE. Dr. J. M'Culloch describes it thus, "about $1\frac{1}{2}$ mile in diameter and rising into a sort of inclined table land of about 300 feet in elevation. Handa forms one of those singular detached portions of sandstone in which this coast abounds; being separated by a space of 7 miles from the nearest mass of the same rock." The soil of Handa is sandy, and unsuitable for cropping purposes. At one time 10 or 12 crofter families lived on it, and paid in 1793 a joint yearly rent of £12. About 30 years ago, all the people of Handa, save one woman, emigrated to America. The island is now under sheep and rabbits. The rabbits, unknown on the isle until about 14 years ago, are now so numerically strong, that the sheep shall soon be "eaten off." A shepherd lives occasionally in a house on the east side of Handa, where there is also an old graveyard. Before the extinction of wolves in Scotland, the sea coast islands were largely used as burying places. The bodies were thus protected from the prowling wolf. A trip to the west coast of Sutherland is always enjoyable, for the wild grandeur of the mountain and loch scenery is unsurpassed in any part of Scotland. The green patches of the fisherman's croft, the yellow whin bushes, the bold cliffs, the majestic hills, and the deep blue of sea and sky, are seen to the best advantage in the lovely month of June. Mr. Lumsden says—"we left Lochinver on the 11th June, 1883, to drive to Scourie, our object being to visit Handa; to see what we could of its bird life, and if possible to take some photos of the rocks, and of birds on their nests. The drive from Lochinver to Scourie is full of interest. The first part is along the river Inver, then up Loch Assynt, at the upper end of which we were near the old ruin of Ardvrach Castle, the home of the osprey in bygone days; then across the ferry at Kyle Sku." Having reached Scourie Inn, kept by Mr. Turnbull, a boat and experienced men, were got to ferry the party across to Handa. "As we got near the island," continues Mr. Lumsden, "we saw Cormorants, Shags, Gulls, and Terns flying about. Quite near the landing place we saw a bird I could not have identified myself with certainty, but which the boatmen called the 'Dirty Allan,' and described its habits, saying that it followed the Gulls and Terns and made them disgorge the fish they had eaten. This graphic description confirmed me in my belief that it was a Richardson Skua." In walking across the island several Wheatears and other small birds were seen. Nearly all the available shelves in the cliffs of the rocks were filled with sea birds—Guillemots, Razorbills, and Puffins. There is on Handa a most interesting well or spouting cave, called Port Luib, about 100 yards deep, by about 30 broad. It goes right down to the sea, by which it is connected by two Gothic shaped arches. But by far the most interesting bit of Handa is the Stack, which simply swarms with bird life, its sides during the nesting season being covered with Razorbills, Guillemots, Puffins and Gulls. After securing a few specimens of eggs, and disturbing a White-tailed

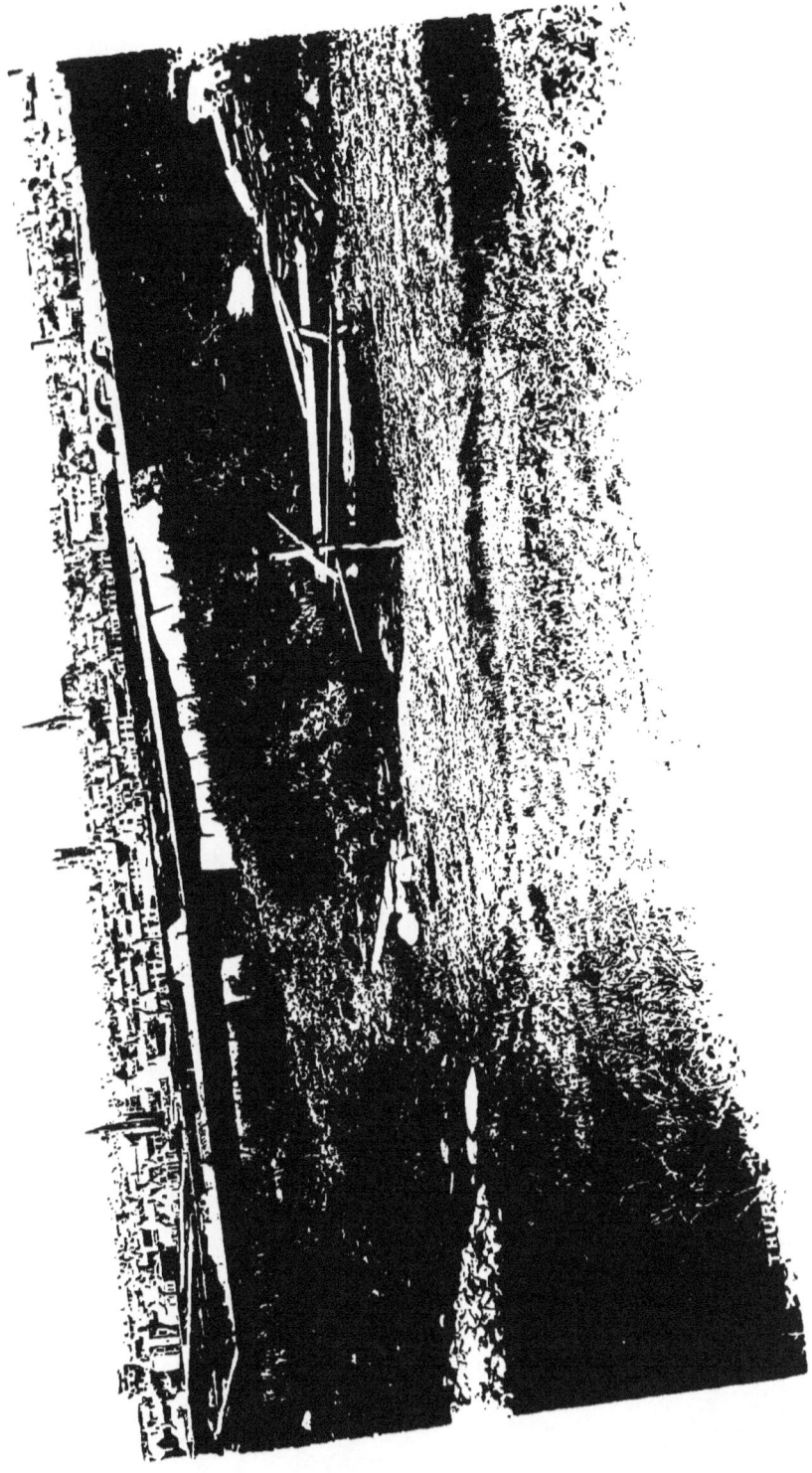

Eagle, the boat was on its way to Scourie. Next day being bright and clear they went back to Handa, accompanied by the ladies of the party. On this occasion they had a pleasant walk along the cliffs, of which a few photos were taken. To sail round Handa and see the many thousands of Guillemots, Razorbills, and Puffins which crowd the outer crags, is a memorable sight.

Mr. M'Iver, Scourie, describes Handa as interesting to geologists. "Its formation is different from that of the mainland opposite, being composed of Sandstone and Conglomerate, while the mainland is of Gneiss and primitive rock. It rises gradually from its southern side on the Sound of Handa to its northern extremity, when it falls perpendicularly to the sea, a height of about 400 feet, and is one of the finest cliffs on the West Coast of Scotland. The ledges of the rocks in the summer months are full of Guillemots and other sea fowl, which nestle there in thousands."

The following is a list of the birds that may be seen on Handa :—

White-tailed Eagle, Peregrine, Wheatears, Tern, Great Black-backed Gull, Lesser Black-backed Gull, Herring Gull, Kittiewake, Razorbill, Richardson's Skua, Guillemot, Puffin, Cormorant, Shag, Oyster Catchers, Petrels, Herons, and Curlews.

After rounding Cape Wrath, the steamer passes the Smoo Cave, Durness; and on leaving Loch Eribol a good view is obtained of the caves of Whiten Head, and on approaching Scrabster (the landing place for Thurso) the Clett, a huge detached rock about 300 feet high, is seen. On looking to the left the Orkney Islands are seen, with the old man of Hoy on the westerly point of Hoy Island.

Thurso, the most northerly town in Scotland, is situated about 1½ miles from Scrabster; it has about 4000 inhabitants, is clean, and contains many neat freestone houses and a handsome church. In the east of it stands a fine old castle (Sir Tollemache Sinclair), and on the west side of the bay are the ruins of the bishop's castle. The distance from Thurso to John o' Groat's House is 21 miles, there is a good road all the way, passing through a beautiful fertile country. About 2 miles from John o' Groat's House are the Stacks at Duncansbay Head, which are well worth a visit, and the district around is of great interest to geologists.

CIRCULAR TOUR.
GLASGOW to OBAN via LOCHAWE.
By Columba or Iona daily, during July, August and September.
FARE FOR THE ROUND: CABIN & 1st CLASS, 22s. 6d.; STEERAGE & 3rd CLASS, 17s. 6d.

	TO OBAN via Lochawe RETURNING via Crinan			TO OBAN via Crinan RETURNING via Lochawe	
	From	A.M.		From	A.M.
STR. COACH STEAMER	{ Glasgow ....at	7 0	STEAMER	{ Glasgow ....at	7 0
		P.M.			P.M.
	{ Ardrishaig...... „	12 40		{ Ardrishaig...... „	12 40
STR. RAIL STR. COACH	{ Ardrishaig...... „	12 50	'LINNET'	{ Ardrishaig...... „	1 0
	{ Ford .... „	3 0		{ Crinan .... „	2 55
	{ Ford .... „	3 0	STR. RAIL STR.	{ Crinan .... „	3 0
	{ Lochawe Pier... „	5 10		{ Oban .... „	4 45
	{ Lochawe Station „	5 15			A.M.
	{ Oban .... „	6 15		{ Oban .... „	8 5
		A.M.		{ Lochawe Station „	9 4
	{ Oban .... „	8 0		{ Lochawe Pier... „	9 5
	{ Crinan .... „	10 0		{ Ford .... „	10 40
'LINNET'	{ Crinan .... „	10 0	STR. COACH	{ Ford .... „	10 45
		P.M.			P.M.
	{ Ardrishaig...... „	12 15		{ Ardrishaig...... „	12 40
STR.	{ Ardrishaig...... „	1 0	STR.	{ Ardrishaig...... „	1 0
	{ Glasgow .... „	6 45		{ Glasgow .... „	6 45

The times stated above are merely given for general information and are NOT guaranteed.

The well-known "Royal Route" to Oban is from Ardrishaig by way of Crinan, but this new route, namely, from Ardrishaig by way of Loch Awe, forms a variety for the tourist. (For description of route, Glasgow to Ardrishaig, see pages 17 to 25). Arriving at Ardrishaig by the Steamer "Columba" or "Iona," a coach is in readiness, which proceeds to Ford, at the south-end of Loch Awe, a distance of about 14 miles. Notably, on the way to Ford, we pass Kilmichael-Glassary, in which valley, at Kirnan, stood "the home of the forefathers," of Thomas Campbell, the poet, referred to in his exquisite "Lines on Visiting a Scene in Argyleshire." The still more charming valley of Kilmartin is afterwards reached, with its wood-clad slopes, its neat village, its handsome parish church, and its ancient castle, the whole forming, perhaps, one of the most picturesque combinations to be witnessed anywhere, in Scotland. A mile further on, Carnassarie Castle crowns a neighbouring height, and having run through Craiginturie Pass with its bold acclivities, and skirted Dog's Head Loch, and Ederline

Loch, we arrive in sight of **Loch Awe**, where the steamer is waiting to convey us to Loch Awe Pier, at the north end of the Lake, a distance of nearly thirty miles.

Ford Loch Awe

The quiet loveliness of the lake cannot fail to please the eye, while of its numerous islands, of which there are twenty-four, not a few have their stories of love and revenge, of pious labours and daring deeds, of which the remains of castles and monasteries are the crumbling memorials. Fionchairn, Innis Erreth, Innes Coulin, Innishail, and Fraoch Eilan, have each of them, in these respects, much to interest the tourist; but chiefly so Innis Connel, with the ruins of Inchconnel Castle, the ancient seat of the lords of Loch Awe, and afterwards of the earls of Argyll. After passing **Port Sonnachan**, and as we approach the north end of the lake, the view becomes imposingly magnificent. The water, which hitherto has been scarcely a mile in breadth, expands in width to about three or four miles, and is enclosed by majestic mountains, among which the massive form of Ben Cruachan is supremely conspicuous; between these are seen the openings of Glenstrae and Glenorchy, and the monument to Duncan Ban M'Intyre, the highland bard, appears on a distant elevation, while nearer are the noble ruins of Kilchurn Castle. We now approach the magnificent pass of Brander, with its precipitous rocky sides, from which the river Awe begins its impetuous course. At Loch Awe Station we quit the steamer, and from this the journey to Oban, about sixteen miles further off, is completed by train, which runs by way of Taynuilt, along the shores of Loch Etive, passing Inverawe Castle, Ossian's "Falls of Lora," and Dunstaffnage Castle, the residence of the early Scottish kings. The mere names of these places are themselves abundantly suggestive of how much there is in the trip to reward all lovers of the picturesque. We arrive in **Oban** at a convenient hour in the evening, and it is but the simple truth to say, that for variety of beautiful and impressive scenery, for delightful interchange of hill and glen, wood and water, lake and mountain, the route is unrivalled, even in the Highlands; while history, tradition, and poetry have invested many of the localities with the richest associations.

Port Sonnachan

Oban

GLASGOW TO ISLAY (via Tarbert).

	GLASGOW TO ISLAY.		A.M.	ISLAY TO GLASGOW.			A.M.
	FROM			FROM			
"COLUMBA" OR "IONA."	Glasgow (Daily April till October) at		7 0	Port-Ellen (Daily except Tuesday) at			8 30
	Greenock (Daily during the Year) ,,		9 0	Port-Askaig (Every Tuesday)			8 30
	Prince's Pier ,, ,,		9 3				
	Kirn ,, ,,		9 25	Gigha (South end, Daily except Tuesday, North end, Every Tuesday)	Daily if Ferry boat is out		10 5
	Dunoon ,, ,,		9 35				
	Innellan ,, ,,		9 50				
	Rothesay ,, ,,		10 15	Clachan Ferry			10 40
	Colintraive ,, ,,		10 40	Ardpatrick Ferry			
	Tignabruaich ,, ,,		10 55	Dunmore Ferry			10 55
	Tarbert (east) ,, ,,		11 45	Tarbert (west)		,,	11 25
COACH	{ Tarbert (east) ,, about		11 50	{ Tarbert (west) daily about			11 30
	{ Tarbert (west),, ,,		12 35p	{ Tarbert (east) ,, ,,			12 5p
"SWIFT STEAMER."	Tarbert (west) ,,	Daily if Ferry boat is out	12 40	Tarbert (east) ,, ,,			1 40
	Dunmore Ferry		1 10	Tignabruaich ,, ,,			2 40
	Ardpatrick Ferry }			Colintraive ,, ,,			3 0
	Clachan Ferry }		1 25	Rothesay ,, ,,			3 30
	Gigha (South end, Daily except Monday, North End Every Monday)		2 0	Innellan ,, ,,			3 50
				Dunoon ,, ,,			4 10
				Kirn ,, ,,			4 15
	ARRIVING AT			Prince's Pier ,, ,,			4 45
	Port-Ellen (Daily except Monday) about		3 40	Greenock ,, ,,			4 50
				ARRIVING AT			
	Port-Askaig (Every Monday),,		8 30	Glasgow ,, ,,			6 45

For Fares see page 5.

This route is already described as far as Tarbert at pages 17 to 24 inclusive. On landing from steamer *East Tarbert* "COLUMBA" or "IONA" at Tarbert, there are coaches waiting to convey passengers and their luggage to West Tarbert, the distance being fully a mile. On leaving the pier a drive of half-a-mile brings us into the village. Before entering it, on our left are seen the ruins of "Tarbert Castle," once the royal residence of King Robert Bruce, already noticed at page 24. As it stands keeping guard over the village it recalls many memories and traditions to the mind. This is the only ancient Castle in Scotland, of the building of which a complete history is now extant. In 1315, after the departure for Ireland of Edward the King's brother, Bruce visited the Isles, and had his galleys drawn across the isthmus of Tarbert. Within ten years of this visit to the Isles, the erection of Tarbert Castle was commenced. There is some evidence of its being left in an unfinished state; or, if really completed, it must have at a later date been partially destroyed. In 1326 the King resided in it, and in this same year John de Lany was Constable of Tarbert and King's Chamberlain for the district. It appears that he paid all the accounts to the different tradesmen employed at the erection of the Castle, the total amount of which was £479 9s. 9½d. We also find a very curious item in the account paid to Sir Maurice, the Chaplain, for his half-year's salary, £2 0s. 0d. The Chamberlain's own salary had been, for one year and sixty-six days, £39 3s. 10½d. We find residing at the Castle at different periods distinguished people, such as the Bishop of St. Andrew's, Sir James, Lord of Douglas; and in 1335, John Earl of Moray, Guardian of Scotland during the time he was negotiating with "John of the Isles," who favoured the English interest. The village itself was at one time the seat of the Scottish Parliament, and a Sheriffdom, but is now inhabited by a hardy race of fishermen. It has several hotels, a bank, and a postal and telegraph office.

As we emerge from the village, on our left is the Established Church, and on our right the Manse. The surrounding country looks rather bare and bleak, but a little further on, as we begin to descend into a glen or valley, the aspect of the country completely changes from the barren to the beautiful. We now pass Cairnbaan and come into full view of Lochend, and the head of the loch with hills crowned with trees rising on both sides, and at their base cultivated fields studded with habitations. This scene, and others similar about Tarbert, afford great and varied study to artists, many of whom come to the place every year in prosecution of their art. The distance between Lochfyne and West Loch Tarbert being only about a mile-and-a-half, the ground has been surveyed on several occasions, with the object of cutting a canal to join the two seas, in order to save vessels the circuit of the "Mull," but the project never came to anything.

West Loch Tarbert is about 9 miles in length, and as will be observed, very shallow at the head. There can be no doubt, as historians inform us, that "Hakon the Old," and "Magnus Barefoot" had their boats taken from this loch across to Lochfyne—the former when on

his way to the Battle of Largs, and from this mode of conveying boats across the isthmus, Tarbert got its name, the derivation being from "tarruing bhàta," or draw boat. The great historian, Carlyle, describes the passage of Hakon the Old across the isthmus in these words:—
"While his ships and army were doubling the Mull of Kintyre, he had his own boat set on wheels, and therein, splendidly enough, had himself drawn across the Promontory, at a flatter part, no doubt with horns sounding and banners waving. 'All to the left of me is mine and Norway's,' exclaimed Hakon, in his triumphant boat progress, which such disasters soon followed."

The Oxford Professor of Poetry, too, has a fine passage regarding this in his "Kilmahoe."

> Then Norroway kings, our chiefs o'erthrown,
> Held isle and islet for their own,
> And one, more haughty than the rest,
> Swore he would claim for island ground
> Whate'er he drove his galley round;
> And from the Atlantic, up the west
> Loch Tarbert bearing, made them haul,
> His barge accoss that isthmus small;
> Himself, proud-seated at the helm.
> Then spreading sail down fair Lochfyne,
> He cried aloud, "Kintyre is mine,
> I've bound it to my island realm."

Our road runs along the side of the loch, and is the highway to Campbeltown. As we ascend a little hill we see the steamer immediately below us, with steam up and ready to start. After passengers embark the bell is rung for dinner, and full justice can be done to it without much fear of being disturbed by the rolling of the vessel, as the loch is quite calm at all times. On our left we pass Carrick Point, where the loch widens out before us, and immediately below this point we notice, on our right, a beautiful little island, Eilein dà Laggan, *(the island of two hollows)*. We now have a full view of this picturesque loch, with all its surroundings, and it is not too much to say that for beauty it has few equals in the Highlands of Scotland. There, rises before us an amphitheatre of grassy pyramidal hills, covered with trees of various hues and shades, and before us lies a loch as still and beautiful as any that imagination can paint. The hills rise up, summit behind summit, in grand array. On our right we pass **Dunmore** House (Miss Campbell), nestling among the trees. We are now in the widest part of the loch. All the way down on our right is Knapdale, and on our left is Kintyre, with the road to Campbeltown visible running along the shore. On our right is Ardpatrick House (Captain Campbell, R.N.), and on our left **Clachan Ferry**, where a boat comes out to meet the steamer; there is also a ferry here from Kintyre to Knapdale. As we sail along we pass Train Island on our right, and directly opposite, on the Kintyre side, is Clachan, and rising behind it we see "Dunskeig," having on its summit a circular fort, 15 yards in diameter, composed of dry stones, and a little below it, at a distance of about 60 yards, is a vitrified fort, 21 yards in diameter, but of an irregular form. It is said to have been used by the Norwegians as a watch-tower and fortress. Straight before us lies the Island of **Gigha**, the property of J. W. Scarlett, Esq., where a boat comes out to meet the steamer. Gigha may be said to comprise three islands, viz., Gigha, Cara, and Giglum. In 1570 King James IV. presented Angus M'Kane to the rectory of the church of Saint Catan, which stood on the east side of the island, near the head of Ardminish Bay. There is said to have been on the Island of Cara a cell to the Holy Trinity, but by whom founded is uncertain. Historians say that in 1263, Haco, King of Norway, in his expedition against Scotland, arrived at Gigha, and there met King John of the Isles, who refused to break his allegiance with the King of Scots. He also met the Abbot of a monastery of Grey Friars (supposed to be Saddell in Kintyre) begging for protection for their church and dwelling, which Haco granted to them in writing. From this island he sent a party to plunder Kintyre, who, after burning some villages, killing some of the inhabitants, and carrying away all the booty they could, returned to the island. There is near Kilchattan (on Gigha) a square artificial mound, with vestiges of a breast wall at the top, similar to the mount called Romelborg, in Sweden. As we skirt the north end of the Island we see on our right the Knapdale hills and shore as far as Crinan, and, looming in the distance, the mountains of Mull; and in the middle of the Sound of Jura the Iron-Rock Light-house. Now we obtain the finest possible view of the Paps of Jura, towering their lofty heads against the western horizon—a scene strikingly depicted by A. H. Clough—

> "And so from Oban's little land-locked bay
> Forth out to Jura—Jura, pictured high,
> With lofty peaks against the western sky;
> Jura, that far o'erlooks the Atlantic sea,
> The loftiest of the Southern Hebrides."

The Paps rise into four distinct hills, the three principal ones being Beinn-an-oir (or mountain of gold), 2,569 feet; Beinn-a-Chaolais (or mountain of sounds), 2,412 feet; and Beinn-Shiannta, the Sacred Mountain.

We are now sailing S.W., and on our right is seen MacArthur's Head and Light-House, overlooking the entrance to the Sound of Islay. This Sound is about 11 miles long, and divides Islay and Jura; about the middle of the Sound is Port-Askaig, where the swift steamer makes a call on the Mondays. South of MacArthur's Head, and on our right, is Proaig Bay, and a little farther down is Ardmore Point. Being now in mid-channel, we have Kintyre on our left and Islay on our right. One has here a good view of the Kintyre shore down to the point of the Mull. The first house seen is Ronachan House (John Pollok, Esq.); close by it is Largie Castle (Mrs. Moreton MacDonald); a little below is the village of Tayinloan, and Killean (J. Hall, Esq.); we also see Cruibosdale (Major MacAlister), and Glen Crigg (the estate of Colonel Eddington), and farther on is Glen Barr Abbey, the beautiful residence of Keith MacAlister, Esq. On Passing Ardmore Point there opens up to us as fine a panorama of scenes as nature could show. Here we have the first proper view of the Mull of Kintyre, standing boldly out against the sky. A few miles from the head of the "Mull" is Machrahanish Bay, with its beautiful shore, where the sea is never at rest, wave following upon wave, and breaking with a roar that can be heard for miles around. In the following almost weird-like lines, befitting the naturally sombre and monotonous character of the place, the visitor will recognize the truth of Principal Shairp's description—

> "And no sound was heard, save only
> Distance—lulled the Atlantic roar.
> Over the calm mountains coming
> From far Machrahanish shore,
> Like an audible eternity
> Brooding the hushed people o'er."

If the weather be favourable, a fine view of the North of Ireland is now to be had; and away in the far distance we see Fair-Head and the hills about Ballycastle. Straight before us is the Island of Rathlin, from which Bruce started on his expedition against the English, which resulted in the decisive victory of Bannockburn. Having now left Ardmore Point behind us, we pass on our right Kildalton, the splendid mansion of John Ramsay, Esq., M.P. for the Falkirk Burghs, beautifully situated, and surrounded by trees. Near Kildalton is an ancient burying-ground, "where the rude forefathers of the hamlet sleep," and where can be seen very fine specimens of early sculpture. There is standing in the middle of the burial-ground an Iona cross in good preservation. We next pass Ardemersay Point, and Ardbeg Distillery (A. M'Dougall & Co.) The island on our left, Texa, is about a mile in length, and tradition says that it was at one time inhabited by monks. On our right, and opposite this island, is the village of Lagavulin, and Distillery (J. L. Mackie & Co.) We observe in the bay, standing on a large peninsular rock, the remains of the ancient castle of Dunyvig, or Dun Naomhaig, a round tower of stones, protected on the land side by a thick earthern mound, beyond which are the ruins of several houses, separated from the main building by a strong wall. It was once a seat of the Lords of the Isles, and in 1400 John Mor of the Isles was styled after Dunyvig and the Glens in Antrim. Below the village, the Established Church and Manse are seen, and a little farther on Laphroaig Distillery appears The hill that stands out in front of us is the Mull of Oa. Entering the harbour we pass on our left the Light-House, built by the late W. F. Campbell of Islay, to commemorate the death of his wife, Lady

Port-Ellen

Eleanor Campbell. A little to the north of the Light-House is Kilnaughton churchyard, and as we approach the pier we see on the hill above the village the Free Church and Manse. Port-Ellen is prettily situated upon the shore of a sandy bay. On landing, omnibuses are waiting to convey passengers and luggage to Bridgend and Bowmore. Port-Ellen has about 1,000 inhabitants, one Church (Free), one Bank, a Postal and Telegraph Office, two Hotels—the Commercial and the White Hart, the latter being the principal. The tourist should, before leaving the island, see the Mull of Oa, the Big Strand, and Slochd Mhaol Doraidh, which can be all accomplished in one day.

On our way to the Mull of Oa we pass on our right the Distillery, and a little beyond it, Colonel Hollin's shooting lodge. Here we obtain a beautiful view of the mountains of Arran, peering their heads above the Kintyre hills. We next pass Cornabus and Kenabus, and twenty minutes' walk from the latter brings us to the Mull of Oa. From the summit of this hill the view is extensive and varied. Beneath is a wide sea, bounded in front by the Irish coast. Away on our left the Giant's Causeway and Port-Rush; on our right Loch Foyle (the entrance to Londonderry), and below it Inshowen Head. To the West there is only one wide expanse of ocean, bounded by the horizon, called the North Channel, and on it can be seen the Atlantic liners and other vessels passing to and fro.

To see from the summit of this hill the sun sinking in the ocean on a summer evening, the sky, with its shifting colours—red, golden, purple, and emerald—the cloudy pinions of the great cherub becoming a magnificent crimson, and again deepening to imperial purple, till the lifeless grey of twilight obscures their glory, is something to be ever remembered.

The summit on which we are standing rises out of the sea to the height of 800 feet; a little below is seen Dun Aidh, with a circular mound and terraces, said to be unique in the Western Isles, and supposed to have been used by the Norwegians as a "thing-place," or seat of judgment.

Our next object of interest—the most remarkable in

the island—is Slochd Mhaol Doraidh. There is no hing very striking in its appearance from the shore until we reach the spot, which is on the west side of the peninsula of Oa, and at the entrance of Lochindaal. In formation it resembles some of the caves in Staffa. As we arrive at the end of the rock we find a circular hole about twenty feet in diameter, with a depth of seveial hundred feet, penetrating through the solid rock, down to the level of the sea. Through this cavern, when the swell from the Atlantic comes in, the water is sent in spray through the opening in the rock with terrific force and noise. There is a cave below, into which a boat can enter. Inside this cave is a large hall, the roof resembling the dome of a cathedral. Two smaller caves branch off this one, which, to be seen, require artificial light. At the entrance to the cave, and, as if guarding the pass, stands a huge pillar of rock, about fifty feet in height, and about ten feet in diameter, called *The Soldier*, from a band of lighter coloured rock which crosses it somewhat diagonally, and is supposed to resemble a soldier's belt. The rocks are fashioned into many fantastic shapes and forms, doubtless by the irresistible power of the sea. Does not Shelley bring home to us the meaning—the inner secret of the Ocean, and the impression it makes on the human heart when he speaks of the—

> "Unfathomable Sea, whose waves are years,
>   Ocean of Time, whose waters of deep woe,
> Are brackish with the Salt of human tears;
>   Thou shoreless flood, which in thy ebb and flow,
> Claspest the limits of mortality,
>   And sick of prey, yet howling on for more,
> Vomitest thy wrecks, on its inhospitable Shore;
>   Treacherous in Calm, and terrible in Storm,
> Who shall put forth on thee, Unfathomable Sea?"

On our way back we get a good view of the Big Strand, a beautiful sandy beach, that runs up Lochindaal-side for several miles, and upon which, after a gale, the Atlantic rollers break, in most magnificent array.

The tourist should make Bridgend (11 miles from Port Ellen) his residence, as the hotel accommodation is very good, and he will also find it more central as a starting point, from which to visit the different places of interest.

The drive to it leads across a long stretch of moor, passing on the way Leorin and Nerby. About half-way on our right, at the foot of Beinn Mhain, is a lake which contains a somewhat strange freak of nature. viz., tail-less trout. As we approach Bridgend, we have a fine view of Lochindaal. The village, beautifully situated at the head of Lochindaal, and nestling among trees, has an air of quiet loveliness about it. It commands good views of the surrounding scenery, and we see on the east side of the loch, about three miles distant, the village of Bowmore. Tours can be made from here to the Rhinns, the southern part of the island. The distance is about twenty miles, and the road skirts the shores of the beautiful Lochindaal, passing on the way the villages of Port-Charlotte, Port-na-haven and Port-Wemyss. About half way down the loch, on our right, is Bruchladich Pier, where the steamer "Islay" calls weekly. The view from the Rhinns is very fine.

Lochgruineart, about seven miles from Bridgend, should next be seen. This loch indents the island for several miles in a northerly direction. In 1598, at the head of Lochgruineart, was fought one of the frequent battles between the Macdonalds and Macleans, in which there was slain on the one side Sir Lachlan Maclean and about 300 of his men, and on the other only about 30 of the Macdonalds. Tradition says that on that occasion the Church of Kilnave, in which some of the Macleans had taken refuge, was burned by the Macdonalds, and that Sir Lachlan Maclean was buried in the Church of Kilchoman. Our next tour is to **Port-Askaig**, which is about nine miles from Bridgend. On our way we pass Islay House (B. H. Newman, Esq.), Ballygrant and the Isle of Finlagan.

Port-Askaig

The Island, which is about three acres in extent, has many features of historical interest, being once the chief seat of the Lords of the Isles; and the ruins of the Castle are still to be seen. On the shore are traces of a pier and of the houses of the *Luchd-tach*, or guards who attended the Lords of the Isles. These Chieftains had their wives and children buried on the island, while their own remains were taken to Iona for interment. The island has a further interest, as being the place in which the Lords of the Isles were installed, and a manuscript history of the Macdonalds, written in the reign of Charles the Second (1649-1685), gives the following interesting account of the installation ceremony. "At this, the Bishop of Argyll, the Bishop of the Isles, and seven priests were sometimes present, with the chieftains of all the principal families, and a *Ruler of the Isles*. There was a square stone seven or eight feet long, and the track of a man's feet cut thereon, upon which he stood, denoting that he should walk in the footsteps and uprightness of his predecessors, and that he was installed by right in his possessions. He was clothed in a white habit to show his innocence and integrity of heart, and that he would be a light to his people, and maintain the true religion. The white apparel did afterwards belong to the poet by right. Then he was to receive a white rod in his hand, intimating that he had power to rule, not with tyranny and partiality, but with discretion and sincerity. Then he received his forefathers' sword, or some other sword, signifying that his duty was to protect and defend them from the incursions of their enemies in peace or war, as the obligations and customs of his predecessors were.

"The ceremony being over, mass was said after the blessing of the bishop and seven priests, the people pouring their prayer for the success and prosperity of the new created lord. When they were dismissed the Lords of the Isles feasted them for a week, and gave liberally to the monks, poets, bards, and musicians. The constitution or government of the Isles was thus:—Macdonald's council sat on this island of Finlagan, and consisted of sixteen in number, and were composed of four thanes, four armins, that is to say, lords or sub-thanes; four squires, or men of competent estates who could not come up with armies or thanes; four freeholders, or men who had their lands in factory. There was a table of stone on the island, where this council met; this table, with the stone on which Macdonald sat, were carried away by Argyll."

Reading this we seem to hear the words of the poet— "Yet a few years and the winds of the desert will howl through thy empty courts."

Having left Finlagan behind, a short drive brings us

to Port-Askaig. Before descending the hill which leads to the hotel we obtain a view of lonely Colonsay, lying away out in the sea on our left. We have also a fine view of the Sound of Islay, and straight opposite us, the Paps of Jura. We see below us the beautiful mansion of Kirkman Finlay, Esq., overlooking the Sound.

Port-Askaig   Port-Askaig is charmingly situated in a nook in the Sound of Islay, and has a comfortable Hotel. There is a ferry from Port-Askaig to Jura, and from this place the ascent of the Paps is easily made. The tourist can return from here on the Tuesday mornings (*via* Tarbert), and from Port-Ellen on the other days of the week.

If there be a desire to vary the route, it can be done by taking the steamer "Islay," which sails from Port-Askaig every Friday forenoon (*via* Port-Ellen and Mull of Kintyre), and on Tuesday and Friday evenings from Port-Ellen round the Mull of Kintyre to Greenock and Glasgow.

To the geologist, Islay affords a fine field for study; to the antiquarian it is of the highest interest, for it abounds in numberless objects of interest; to the lovers of the beautiful in nature it will be found to compare favourably with any island in Scotland. For historic interest it cannot be surpassed, and we know of no place where a few days can be more pleasantly spent away from the toils of busy life, than here.

The *CALEDONIAN RAILWAY COMPANY*

Issue Tourist Tickets to Ardrishaig, Oban, Inverness, Skye, Islay, &c., in connection with the Steamers at Greenock from Carlisle, Dumfries, Edinburgh, Glasgow, Paisley, Stirling, Perth, Dundee, Aberdeen, and other Stations. For Train Service and Fares, *see* that Company's Time Tables and Tourist Guides which are procurable on board, or at the Stations of the Company.

The *NORTH BRITISH RAILWAY COMPANY*

Issue Tourist Tickets to Ardrishaig, Oban, Inverness, Skye, Islay, &c., in connection with the Steamers at Glasgow and Dunoon, from Newcastle, Morpeth, Hexham, Carlisle, Peebles, Melrose, Galashiels, Edinburgh, Glasgow, Perth, Dundee, Arbroath, Aberdeen, and other Stations. For Train Service and Fares, *see* the North British Company's Time Tables and Tourist Programme, which can be obtained on board the Steamers, or at the Stations of the Company.

The *GLASGOW & SOUTH-WESTERN RAILWAY CO.*

Issue Tourist Tickets to Ardrishaig, Oban, Inverness, Islay, &c., *via* Kyles of Bute, from Glasgow (St. Enoch), Paisley, Kilmarnock, Ayr, Dumfries, and Carlisle. For particulars as to Train Service and Fares, *see* that Coy's Tourist Programme, which can be obtained on board or at the office of the Superintendent of the Line, Saint Enoch Station, Glasgow.

TOURS TO THE WEST HIGHLANDS.

(Occupying about a Week).

BY STEAM SHIP
"CLAYMORE" or "CLANSMAN,"
GLASGOW TO MULL, SKYE, STORNOWAY & BACK.

(Via Mull of Kintyre.)

WITH GOODS AND PASSENGERS

Every Monday and Thursday throughout the year, except about January or February, when the Mondays' Steamer from Glasgow may be withdrawn.

CABIN RETURN FARE, 45s.

Breakfast, Dinner, and Tea, 7s. per day.

Passengers continuing the voyage to THURSO and back pay 10s. extra fare. (For description of route, Stornoway to Thurso, see page 75.)

NOTE.—*Passengers by the Swift Steamers Columba or Iona on Monday and Thursday via Crinan Canal to Oban (from May till October) may join the Claymore or Clansman, there on Tuesday and Friday Mornings not earlier than 8 o'clock.*

FROM	Clansman. Monday. p.m.	Claymore. Thursday. p.m.	FROM	Clansman Wednesday p.m.	Claymore. Monday. p.m.
Glasgow. about	1 0	1 0	Stornoway...ab	10 0p	1 0p
Greenock ..,, }	5 0	5 0			
Cus. Ho. Pier }	Tuesday.	Friday.			
Oban ......,,..	8 0a	8 0a			
Craignure.,,..	9 0	9 0			
Lochaline .,,..	9 30	9 30			
Salen......,,..	10 30	10 30			
Tobermory,,..	12 0	12 0			
Eigg ......,,..	——	1 30p		Thursday	Tuesday
Arisaig..,,..	2 0p	——	Portree ....,,	6 0a	4 0a
Inverie...,,..	——	——	Raasay ....,,	6 30	4 30
Armadale.,,..	3 30	3 0	Broadford ..,,	7 35	5 30
Isle Orusay,,..	——	4 30	Kyleakin....,,	8 10	6 0
Glenelg ...,,..	5 20	5 15	Balmacara ..,,	8 25	6 30
Balmacara ,,..	5 50	6 0	Glenelg......,,	9 0	7 15
Kyleakin..,,..	6 0	6 30	Isle Orusay..,,	——	8 0
Broadford .,,..	6 40	7 30	Armadale...,,	10 5	8 45
Raasay .....,,..	——	8 30	Inverie......,,	10 40	——
Portree...,,..	9 0	9 0	Arisaig......,,	——	10 0
	Wednesday.	Saturday.	Eigg ....,,	——	10 30
*Gairloch..,,..	——	6 0a	Tobermory...,,	2 0p	12 5p
*Poolewe..,,..	——	8 0	Salen ....,,	3 0	1 15
*Aultbea..,,..	——	9 30	Lochaline....,,	3 35	2 0
*Ullapool .,,..	6 0a	——	Craignure...,,	4 10	3 0
*Lochinver,,..	6 0	——	Oban ....,,	6 0	4 0
*Lochmaddy..	6 0	——	Cus. Ho. Pier }	Friday	Wedn'sday
*Harris ..,,..	9 0	——	Greenock arr }	6 0a	6 0a
Stornoway arr	5 0p	1 0p	Glasgow.....,,	9 0	9 0

The hours noted above are not to be absolutely relied upon—they only show about the average sailing time. The Steamer may be earlier or later than what is stated.

* For dates of Call, see Sailing Bill.

Glasgow
Greenock

The trip from Glasgow to Stornoway, by steamship Claymore or Clansman, is a very pleasant one. These vessels leave **Glasgow** every Monday and Thursday about noon, and **Greenock** about 5 P.M. They have excellent passenger accommodation, and parties desirous of enjoying about a week's sail (sleeping on board each night, except on the Thurso trips, when passengers have either to remain at Stornoway till steamers return, or pay 10s. extra fare to Thurso and back), will find them extremely comfortable. The route is *via* Mull of Kintyre, Sounds of Jura, Mull, and Skye, passing through the most beautiful scenery in the West Highlands. After leaving Greenock the steamer sails down the Firth of Clyde, passing the Cumbrae islands (left), and the Island of Bute (right). Sailing along the shores of Arran, its bold and dark-blue mountains pass in grand review before our gaze. The little island adjoining Arran, and which we might suppose was part of it, is the Holy Isle. Immediately behind this island is Lamlash Bay. We now pass close to Pladda Lighthouse, and steer our course for the Mull.

On our left, about seven miles off, can be seen the famous Ailsa Craig, towering high above the sea level, and seemingly proud of its solitary position. It is the haunt of innumerable sea fowl. In the distance, looking to the right, can be seen the faint yet clear flickering of Davaar light, which is placed on a little island at the entrance of Campbeltown harbour. A little further on we pass the island of Sanda, on which there is a lighthouse, and in about three-quarters of an hour's sail reach the Mull Lighthouse, after rounding which the course is along the shores of Jura, passing the Iron Rock Lighthouse, and close to the whirlpool of Corryvrechan. On the following morning the steamer approaches the Sound of Kerrera, and shortly thereafter arrives at **Oban**, where passengers can have an hour or two on shore while the vessel is discharging cargo. The time can be spent very pleasantly, as there are many interesting places to visit in the immediate neighbourhood of the town; a description of which will be found on pages 31, 32 and 33.

Oban

Before starting from Oban the steamer's bell is rung three times to give due warning; and on hearing it the first time passengers should get on board again. Emerging from Oban bay the steamer passes on the right the grand old ruin of Dunollie Castle, and on the left the island of Kerrera. The course now steered is across Loch Linnhe, and thence *via* the Sound of Mull to Tobermory, calling at the intermediate ports of Craig- nure, Lochaline and Salen. The detention at these ports is not long, and the entire sail occupies about three hours. There are a number of interesting places in the district, a description of which will be found on pages 55 and 56. We now arrive at Tobermory, the chief town in Mull, which is prettily situated, has two churches, County buildings, and a prison. The steamer usually remains here about an hour or so, according to the amount of cargo to be discharged. Definite information as to time allowed can be had from the purser of the steamer. After leaving Tobermory the steamer steers for the island of Eigg, passing on the left Rhu-na-gael Lighthouse, and on the right Ardnamurchan Point, the most westerly part of the mainland of Scotland. Should the day be clear, a good view is got of the islands of Coll, Muck, Eigg, and Rum. The steamer which leaves Glasgow on Thursdays calls at Eigg. There is moderate hotel accommodation to be had, and the scenery and geology of the island is very interesting. Tourists can proceed by steamer to Loch Coruisk and Skye, or to Oban, or take boat over to Arisaig, on the mainland opposite (at which place the steamer leaving Glasgow on Mondays calls), and drive to Banavie or Fort-William, and thence by steamer to Inverness or Oban. The drive is a magnificent one, the road winding along the shores of Loch Eilt, past the head of Loch Shiel, and by the north side of Locheil to Banavie. At the head of Loch Shiel stands the Monument erected to the memory of Prince Charles Edward Stuart, here being the place where he first unfurled his standard in the Highlands.

After leaving Eigg, the same course is followed for Armadale, Isleornsay, Glenelg, Balmacara, Kyleakin and Broadford as by the steamer for Gairloch. A description of the route will be found on pages 67, 68 and 69. On arriving at Portree, the chief town in Skye, tourists can start for the different places of interest in the island. There are some very good hotels here. For description of route to Stornoway *direct*, see page 99.

PORTREE TO STORNOWAY,

Via Lochmaddy and Tarbert (Harris).

From Portree Bay we enter the Sound of Raasay, and steer our course along the northern shores of Skye, passing the famous Storr Rocks, Kilt Rock, and Quiraing. The islands on our right are Raasay and Rona, and on entering the Minch the "Long Island" appears in view —that group of islands called the Outer Hebrides—the principal of which are Lewis, and Harris, North and South U'st, Benbecula, and Barra; the whole length from Barra Head to the Butt of Lews is 120 miles. The northern part of this great island-chain, viz., the Lews, (40 miles long and in some places 24 in breadth), is in Ross-shire—Harris (though in the same island), and all the other islands, belong to Inverness-shire. Harris is separated from the Lews by a long mountain range of about 8 miles in width, formerly the property of the MacLeods, but now belonging to Lord Dunmore. The whole of North Uist belongs to Sir John P. Campbell Orde, Bart. The islands of Benbecula and South Uist belong to Lady Gordon Cathcart, Cluny, Aberdeenshire.

Lochmaddy. The sail from Portree to Lochmaddy usually occupies about four-and-a-half hours. **Lochmaddy** possesses a number of harbours capable of containing almost any quantity of shipping. As an example of the intricate windings of our salt-water lochs, and the number of islands with which they are studded, we may instance Lochmaddy, which covers about 10 square miles only, and yet the coast line of its numerous windings, creeks, bays, and islands, exceeds 300 miles. Lochmaddy is the principal town of interest in the district, and is the residence of a Sheriff-Substitute.

A packet sails daily between Lochmaddy and Dunvegan in Skye—the distance is 24 miles, and the fare five shillings. Among the many places of interest in North Uist we may mention a large ruin, in good preservation, at Carinish, called *Teampul na Trianaid*, or Trinity Temple, is said to have been erected in the fourteenth century, by Annie M'Rorie, first wife of John of Isla, Lord of the Isles. Among the numerous caves may be mentioned

Slochd-a'-choin, or the cave of the kettle, at the point of Tigharry, not far from the Parish Church of North Uist. In South Uist are the remains of the Castle of Borve, on the west side of Benbecula; the remains of a place of refuge on an islet in Loch Druidibeg; the Castle of Ormaclete, the walls of which are still quite entire, an ancient seat of the chiefs of Clanranald. On a small islet in a lake near Howmore, are the ruins of another castle of the Clanranald; and the remains of *Caisteal-a'-Bhreabadair*, or the Weaver's Castle, perched on a high rock in an island at the southern extremity of South Uist, near Eriscay, and opposite Barra.

The castle in best preservation is in the south end of the island of Barra, at Castlebay, and was the ancient residence of the MacNeill's. The sail from Lochmaddy to Tarbert occupies about two hours and a-half, the route being along the shores of North Uist. After passing the island at Glass Lighthouse, the steamer enters the Sound of Harris, and passes the island of Scalpay. There are a few houses on the island, the inhabitants of which are chiefly engaged in fishing. The Sound of Harris is about 8 miles wide. It is studded with islands, and the navigation is intricate. The village of **Tarbert** (Harris) has good hotel accommodation, and visitors can have plenty of rod-fishing. There is also a Post and Telegraph Office. Here are manufactured the famous "Harris Tweeds," and should the visitor have time, it would well repay his trouble to visit one of the little cots where the cloth is spun. The process of manufacture is simple, the machinery employed rude, yet the cloth, when finished and dressed. will compare favourably with that made in some of our large towns. The ruins of Rodel Monastery are situated on the south-east point of the island, on the sea-coast, under Ben Rowadill; it belonged to the Canons Regular of St. Augustine, and was one of the 28 monasteries in Scotland. The foundations are of Norman design, while the superstructure is of early English. The distance from Tarbert to the march of Lews is 8 miles, and thence to Stornoway 21 miles. The sail from Tarbert to **Stornoway** usually occupies two-and-a-half hours.

<small>Tarbert (Harris)</small>

<small>Stornoway</small>

While the eastern shore of these islands is bleak and sterile, the western shore facing the broad Atlantic, although broken by occasional rocky headlands, is entirely different. There is a large extent of good arable land, consisting of a light, sharp soil, which yields good grain crops, as well as potatoes, turnips, &c. The whole length of the island is now traversed by at least one good road; whilst excellent school-houses have been provided, and the inns improved perhaps as much as can for the present be expected in a locality so remote.

The population of Harris and Bernera is about 4000; North Uist, 4000; South Uist, 5000; Barra, 2000.

PORTREE TO STORNOWAY,
Via Ullapool and Lochinver.

After leaving Portree the steamer resumes her course through the Sound of Raasay, having Skye on the left, and Raasay and Rona Islands on the right. On emerging from the Sound of Raasay we enter the Minch, and steer a north-easterly course along the shores of Ross-shire, passing Loch Torridon and Gairloch. After about three hours' sail from Portree the steamer passes close to Rhu Rea Point, at the entrance of Loch Ewe, and shortly thereafter Greenstone Point, at the entrance of Loch Gruinard, also little Loch Broom, as well as Isle Martin and Priest Island. The shores at the entrance of Loch Broom (the lake of showers) are bold and rocky.

The sail from the mouth of the loch to Ullapool occupies three-quarters of an hour. The scenery is grand, "Ben More," the highest hill in the district, standing out very prominently. At **Ullapool** the steamer goes alongside a safe and substantial pier. The village, founded by the British Fishery Society about eighty years ago, stands on a fine terraced, gravelly promontory, about half-a-mile square, between the loch and the mouth of the river of Achall. The houses are ranged in several parallel lines, and the most conspicuous buildings are the church, manse, and hotel. The hotel accommodation is comfortable, and there is a postal and telegraph office in the village. The inhabitants, in number about 800, are chiefly employed in fishing.

The beach at Ullapool affords good bathing facilities.

In summer the air, although soft, is bracing—the surrounding scenery is often enlivened by the sight of boats and vessels, which come to anchor in the loch. A coach or mail car runs between Garve Station, on the Dingwall and Skye section of the Highland Railway, and Ullapool (distance 32 miles) and *vice versa*, daily during summer, three days a week during winter; and the scenery along this route is very fine. Some miles inland is Loch Achall, the source of the river Ullapool. In the glen through which the river flows there is a waterfall, which is well worth seeing.

Coigach, as the district northward as far as the boundary of Sutherland is called, is exceedingly wild, and the drive along the road from Ullapool to Coigach brings scenery to view of the most magnificent description.

The sail from Ullapool to Lochinver occupies two hours, the route being along the shores of Sutherlandshire, passing the island of Tanera and the Summer Isles.

Approaching Lochinver a series of huge mountain masses are seen—in the distance Cumaig and Ben More (2543 feet); in the centre, Caneshb, (2786 feet), and Suil Bhein, (or the "Sugar Loaf") (2403 feet), and behind Coul More, Coul Beg, and Ben More of Coigach. M'Culloch thus graphically describes the situation of Lochinver :—"Round about there are four mountains, which seem as if they had tumbled down from the clouds, having nothing to do with the country or each other, either in shape, material, position, or character, and which look very much as if they were wondering how they got there."

The village of Lochinver, composed of a few scattered houses, lies at the head of the loch. Culag House is finely situated, close to the sea, on the bay at Lochinver, and until recently it was occupied by the Duke of Sutherland as a shooting lodge. Lochinver Hotel (John Dinnett) has been lately enlarged. Visitors have the privilege of fishing in the rivers Kirkaig and Inver, which are close to the hotel, and afford good sport. There are also several lochs in the immediate neighbourhood, celebrated for the number, variety, and heavy weight of the trout which frequent their waters. The Falls of Kirkaig, five miles from the hotel, are well worthy of a visit. Stoir Lighthouse is six miles off. The scenery around is extremely beautiful, and geologically the neighbourhood of Lochinver is of great interest. It was the frequent resort of Sir Roderick Murchison, Professor Sedgwick, Professor Nicol, of Aberdeen, and other scientific men, and the district has always been a popular resort of tourists, and promises to be much more visited now that the steamboat communication has been so greatly increased.

It is in the option of the captain to call at either Ullapool or Lochinver first. The purser of the steamer will give definite information as to the time the vessel is likely to be detained at the different ports of call.

The steamer again resumes her course, and in about four hours enters the harbour of Stornoway.

PORTREE TO STORNOWAY,
Via Gairloch, Poolewe and Aultbea.

The steamer now passes out of Portree Bay, and enters the Sound of Raasay, where the hills on both sides rise almost perpendicularly from the sea. A description of the route between Portree and Gairloch will be found on pages 70, 71, 72 and 73. The sail between the two ports—Portree and Gairloch—occupies two hours and a quarter. The steamer usually remains at Gairloch, where there is a postal and telegraph office, for about two hours; but the detention entirely depends upon the quantity of cargo to be discharged.

We are again in the Minch; away on our left is seen that group of islands called the "Outer Hebrides," while behind, in the far distance, we see the lofty Cuchullins towering in majestic grandeur. The north end of Skye, in all its rugged beauty, can also be seen; while on our right the noble "Ben Slioch," with the morning sun dispelling the mist from his brow, gazes with pride upon the mirrored sea. The islands on our left, and nearer than Lews, are the Shiant Isles.

Entering Loch Ewe, a number of crofters' houses are seen on the right, with their picturesque stripes of cultivated land; while on the left is Isle Ewe and Aultbea. We now arrive at Poolewe, which is situated at the head of the loch: the village comprises a few slated and thatched houses. There is a good hotel, as well as a postal and telegraph office here. The road from Poolewe to Gairloch passes along the foot of Loch Maree, the distance being six miles. A mail car runs between these places three times a week.

<small>Poolewe</small>

The grandest view of Loch Maree is obtained about a mile from Poolewe, before descending the steep slope of Tolly; the whole length of the loch (18 miles), with the landscape several miles beyond, being visible to the eye. Looking northwards, Loch Ewe, stretching out into the Minch, is seen, with the river Ewe, which connects the two lochs, flowing at its foot. This river separates the properties of Gairloch (Sir Kenneth Mackenzie, Bart.) and Inverewe (Osgood H. Mackenzie, Esq.) Inverewe House is nicely situated amongst a clump of trees on the east side of the loch, and is partly visible from the steamer.

Our next port of call is Aultbea, the sail from Poolewe occupying half an hour. The village is situated on the north-east side of Loch Ewe, the houses being scattered along the sea-beach. Facing Aultbea is Isle Ewe ($1\frac{3}{4}$ miles in length), a very fertile island, on which are a number of houses, and conspicuous amongst them is the farm steading of William Reid, Esq. We now steam out of Loch Ewe, and enter the Minch.

<small>Aultbea</small>

A sail of three hours brings us in sight of Stornoway and passing the lighthouse, we enter one of the finest harbours on the West Coast.

<small>Stornoway</small>

PORTREE TO STORNOWAY, DIRECT.

After about two hours' stay at Portree, the steamer resumes her course along the northern shores of Skye, affording the tourist a view of the famous Storr Rock and Quiraing. After passing the north end of Skye, the Shiant isles, belonging to the Lews, are seen on the left. These islands are of the same geological formation as the northern part of Skye, and different from that of Lews and Harris, and their chief features are the great number of sea birds on them in summer, and the fine

green natural grasses in winter. In the distance, on the
left, are seen the highest hills in the Outer Hebrides—
"Chesham" in Harris (2,600 feet), and "Ben-More" in
Lews (1,600 feet).

As we approach Lews, we can see only rock and
heather on the high ground on our left. The several
sea-lochs that run inland, and the numerous crofter
townships on their edges cannot well be seen from the
steamer. A little further on, the lower ground ahead,
and, on our right, a long, flat-topped hill (Munch, 808
feet), standing towards the north end of Lews, comes
into view. The land nearer, and more to the right, is
the Point of Eye, almost cut off from the rest of Lews,
the breadth at some parts being only 130 yards.

On nearing the lighthouse at Arnish point, tourists
will observe a hollow right ahead, which divides the
conglomerate from the gneiss, and the division runs
almost due north through the middle of Stornoway
Harbour, for about ten miles in a line a little to the east
of Toltsa glen, on the north side of Broadbay.

Stornoway is beautifully situated; Lewis Castle,
on the heights, with its finely laid out grounds, and the
town, bustling with active life, make a very pleasant
picture. The population is about 3,000, and there are
four churches (Established, Free, United Presbyterian,
and Episcopalian), also a Court-house.

The tourist would do well to visit Lewis Castle, in the
immediate neighbourhood. By the approach from Bay-
head Street the distance is half a mile. In the demesne
are ten miles of carriage drives, and five miles of foot
walks. The flatter ground along the principal drive has
been finely planted with trees, and the sharp sloping
ground with grass and plantation alternating. From the
Castle a fine view of the town, harbour, and outlying
districts can be had, with the hills of Ross and Sutherland shires in the distance.

The principal place of interest in the country is
Callernish, where there are a number of druidical stones.
This is one of the favourite places which tourists visit.
Near to Callernish is the little inn of Garry-na-hine, which
Mr. Black describes in his "Princess of Thule." About
16 miles from Stornoway is the famed Loch Grimister.

STORNOWAY (MAIL ROUTE) TO INVERNESS.
Via Strome Ferry.
Daily (to and from) in Summer, and three times weekly in Winter.

PORTREE TO STROME FERRY AND INVERNESS.
Via Raasay, Broadford, Plockton, &c.
Daily during July, August, September, and October, and Three Times Weekly in Wintor.

From	A.M.	From	P.M.
Portree .... at	7 0	Inverness .... at	12 10
Raasay .... about	7 25	Strome Ferry ...... arrive	3 30
Broadford .... ,,	8 30	Do. Steamer leaves	4 0
Plockton .... ,,	9 15	Plockton .. .. about	4 15
Strome Ferry ...... arrive	9 30	Broadford .... ,,	5 0
Do. Train leaves	11 0	Raasay .... ,,	6 5
Inverness .... about	2 30p	Portree .... ,,	6 30

The times stated above are given merely for general information and are NOT guaranteed.

CABIN FARE (Portree to Strome Ferry), 6s. 8d.; RETURN, 10s.

The distance from Portree to Strome Ferry is 30 miles, and the scenery (although the hills in some parts are bare and rugged), is very grand. Tourists returning same day have usually five hours on shore, which allows them ample time to cross the loch and see Strome Castle.

As the steamer sails out of Portree bay into the Sound of Raasay, the tourist will be pleased with the appearance of the very high hills on both sides. On the left the steamer passes **Raasay** the property of Herbert Wood, Raasay Esq. Dr. Johnson and Boswell visited this island on their celebrated tour to the Hebrides. Between Raasay and Scalpa, looking behind, a magnificent view can be had of Loch Sligichan and Loch Ainneart. These lochs are about a mile apart, and the high hills of Glaimaig, with the lofty Cuchullins, make the scene very fine. When the tide is suitable, the steamer passes between the islands of Scalpa and Skye. The hills of Applecross, Lochalsh, and Kintail, are here seen to advantage in the distance. The next calling place is **Broadford**, one of Broadford. the landing places for tourists who wish to visit the Cuchullin hills, Lochs Scavaig and Coruisk. After leaving this, the beautiful fossil-filled island of Pabba is passed on the left, and in front is the long stretch of land-locked water of Lochalsh, with its two inward arms, Loch-Duich and Loch-Long. At Kyleakin many tourists make a short stay, the district being a favourite resort of artists, who admire fine scenery. Here was to have been the terminus of the Skye Railway. There is a comfortable hotel, and good sea fishing can be had. The ruins of Castle Moil stand out prominently to the right of the village. Another half-hour's sail brings us in view of Loch Kishorn, and Loch Carron, and soon after, on the left, the steamer calls at Plockton, and passes Duncraig Castle, the seat of Sir Alex. Matheson, with its picturesque grounds. At this point the loch is studded with numerous islands and rocks, which make the navigation intricate. The coast line on both sides for some distance has, with its numerous gravel terraces, a remarkable appearance. The steamer having reached Strome Ferry, the terminus of the Dingwall and Skye section of the Highland Railway, the ruins of Strome Castle can be seen, and looking towards the head of Loch Carron a good view is got of Jeantown, the principal place in the district. From Strome Ferry (Station Hotel, Mr. Ross), tourists can proceed by a very interesting railway route to Inverness, and steamer *via* Caledonian Canal to Oban or Glasgow, or by Highland or Great North of Scotland Railways to Glasgow. If tourists desire to return to Skye by a different route, the train can be taken to Auchnasheen, coach (*via* Loch Maree) to Gairloch, and steamer to Portree.

Side-notes: Plockton. Strome Ferry.

PORTREE TO INVERNESS.
Via Ullapool and Garve.

The sail from Portree to Ullapool is one of great beauty. An array of mountains, extending over a greater length than can be seen almost anywhere else, is here visible. Northwards they extend to within a few miles of Cape Wrath, and southwards the range extends as far as Loch Maree and Gairloch. The sail from the entrance of Loch Broom to Ullapool occupies about fifty minutes, amongst grand scenery. *Benmore* stands out very prominently on the left, and *Ben Goleach* on the right. Ullapool is situated on a fine terraced promontory, with a beautiful gravelly shore, jutting out on the north side of the loch. There is a good hotel, where passengers can put up before starting by coach for Garve, a station on the Dingwall and Skye Railway—distant 32 miles. The drive from Ullapool to Garve is through most varied scenery, the road for the first eight

Side-note: Ullapool.

miles skirting Loch Broom, and affording the tourist a fine view of this beautiful sea-loch. About half way between Ullapool and the head of the loch, the road passes through the estate of Leckmelm, recently acquired by A. G. Pirie, Esq., who is speedily converting this once neglected looking property into one of great beauty. For some miles from the head of the loch the road runs through flat cultivated land, and rich haughs, covered with grass, and overgrown with hazel and alder, until it reaches a narrow gorge, along the side of which the road rises precipitously for more than a mile, when it reaches the great plateau above—a height of from 500 to 600 feet above the sea. Braemore House, the autumn residence of John Fowler, Esq., C.E. (who has successfully exerted his skill and experience in transforming and embellishing this remote spot), stands on the east side, on the spur of the hill, and overlooks Loch Broom and a noble array of mountains. The steep slope has been planted, and opened up with walks, one of which runs by the side of a remarkable gorge more than a mile in length, called Corry Halloch, and perhaps one of the wildest and most striking to be seen in the West Highlands. The sides rise from the water's edge to a height of from 150 to 200 feet, through flaggy rocks, which appear at one spot like an upright wall, and at another are broken into ledges, and pinnacles. The river falls out of sight, sheer down among the rocks; and following the road, one is only able to catch a glimpse of it now and then by peering over the dangerous precipice. As there is a very steep incline for fully a mile on this part of the road, coach passengers usually walk, and by the kindness of Mr. Fowler, they have the privilege of leaving the county road and of viewing, from the private paths and bridge constructed by Mr. Fowler, this wonderful gorge and the magnificent Falls therein.

The coach is rejoined at the head of the Glen, and from this point the country becomes wild and bare, but the drive is interesting, forming a remarkable contrast with the luxuriant foliage of the former part of the road. Two miles from Braemore, Loch-Druim (or the Ridge Loch) is reached, and the road skirts its banks for a mile and a half, and about half a mile further on, the coach arrives at the summit of the road—it being at this point about 950 feet above the sea-level. Here is the water shed—the one half flowing westward into Loch-Druim and on to Loch-Broom and the Atlantic—the other half, then called the Blackwater, flowing eastward through Loch Garve and on to the German ocean.

The strath is called the *Diridh more*, a name which is, to Highland people, if travelling on a stormy day in winter, synonymous with dreariness. The *Diridh more*, and the adjoining hills are divided between four extensive deer forests Braemore, Strathvaich, Inchbae, and LochLuichart.

As the coach approaches its destination, Loch Garve comes in view. The richness of the variety of woodland scenery along the northern and western shores of this Loch, the delightful situation of the proprietor's lodge (Strathgarve, C. A. Hanbury, Esq.), half hidden in fir and larch plantations, and the Loch itself—a fine sheet of water stretching to about one-and-three quarter miles in length, by three-fourths of a mile in breadth—renders the last portion of the coach journey most interesting and delightful, forming another contrast to the miles of bare, bracing moorland just passed.

Garve is reached about four o'clock, enabling passengers to catch the evening train to Inverness. The railway journey from Garve to Dingwall—12 miles—is most romantic. Looking to the north a passing glimpse is now and then obtained of Ben Wyvis (the mountain of storms), while on the south, the line winds past the Raven Rock, and along the side of Glenskiach, in the bottom of which the Peffery goes rushing down over its rugged, rocky bed.

The train stops at Strathpeffer Station, (four-and-a-half miles from Dingwall). A mile and a half from the station is the celebrated Mineral Spa of Strathpeffer. Passengers having time to spare, would be well repaid by breaking their journey either at Garve or here—the surroundings are very lovely and enjoyable. The Falls of Rogie (on the Blackwater) and many other places of interest are in the locality. The railway from Dingwall to Inverness passes through a rich, arable district, crosses the Rivers Conon and Beauly, and skirts the head of the Cromarty Firth and the south shore of Loch Beauly.

GLASGOW AND THE HIGHLANDS.
ROYAL ROUTE.
(VIA CRINAN AND CALEDONIAN CANALS).

The ROYAL MAIL STEAMER "Columba" or "Iona" sails daily at 7 A.M. (Sunday excepted) from GLASGOW BRIDGE WHARF for Ardrishaig and intermediate places, conveying passengers from

Glasgow to Oban.
Daily, *via* CRINAN, from about middle of May till about middle of October....at 7 A.M.
Also daily via Lochawe during July, August and September at 7 a.m.

Glasgow to Ballachulish, Fort-William and Inverness.
Every Monday, Wednesday, and Friday, till about end of June, daily thereafter till about end of September, and every Monday, Wednesday, and Friday, till about middle of October,...at 7 A.M.

Glasgow to Islay.
Daily, *via* TARBERT at 7 A.M., also from ISLAY daily,......................at 8-30 A.M.

Oban to Glasgow.
Daily *via* CRINAN, from about middle of May till about midddle of October,......at 8 A.M.
Also daily via Lochawe during July, August and September.

Banavie, Fort-William, and Ballachulish to Glasgow.
Every Tuesday, Thursday and Saturday, till about end of June, daily thereafter till about end of Septr, and every Tuesday, Thursday, and Saturday, till about middle of Octr. from Banavie 4-45, Corpach 5-5, Fort-William 5-15, and Ballachulish, at 6-5 A.M.

Inverness to Glasgow.
Every Monday, Wednesday, and Friday, till about end of June, daily thereafter till about end of September, and every Monday, Wednesday and Friday, till about middle of October,...at 7 A.M.

Oban to Loch Scavaig.
Every Tuesday, during July, August, and September,...........................at 7 A.M

Oban to Skye and Gairloch.
Every Tuesday, Thursday and Saturday, during July, August and September....at 7 A.M.

Oban to Staffa and Iona.
Frequently in June, and daily in July, August and September.....................at 8 A.M.

Oban to Ballachulish (Glencoe), Fort-William and Banavie.
Daily during July, August and September, at 6 a.m., 12-45, and 4-50 p.m.; and in May, June and October, daily at 12-45 p.m., and every Monday, Wednesday and Friday at 4-50 p.m.

Oban to Inverness.
Daily in July, Aug., and Sept., at 6 a.m., arriving at Inverness same day; and at 12-45 and and 4-50 p.m., arriving at Banavie same evening, and Inverness the following day.

Glasgow to Oban, Tobermory, Portree and Stornoway.
The CLAYMORE or CLANSMAN, every Monday and Thursday at 12 noon; leaving Stornoway every Monday and Wednesday, and Portree, every Tuesday at 4 a.m., and every Thursday at 6 a.m., for Glasgow. etc. To Thurso on dates advertised.

Portree, Strome Ferry and Inverness.
Calling at Raasay, Broadford, Plockton, &c., daily (to and from) during July, August, September and October, and three times weekly in Winter.

Stornoway (Mail Route) to Inverness and the South.
Via Strome Ferry,
Daily (to and from) in Summer, and three times weekly in Winter.

For Sailings to Arisaig, Isle Ornsay, Inverie (Lochnevis), Aultbea, Poolewe, (Ross-shire,) Loch-maddy and Tarbert (Harris), Ullapool and Lochinver, Thurso, etc. See Bills from
DAVID MACBRAYNE, 119 HOPE STREET, GLASGOW.

Circular Tickets Issued on Board Steamer, and at Oban Railway Station, Cabin and First-Class, **15s.**

GRAND CIRCULAR TOUR.
OBAN & LOCHAWE,
(THIS TOUR CAN BE COMPLETED IN ONE DAY),
Daily during July, August, and September.

	OBAN & ARDRISHAIG. GOING *via Crinan.* RETURNING *via Lochawe.*			OBAN & ARDRISHAIG. GOING *via Lochawe.* RETURNING *via Crinan.*	
	From	A.M.		From	A.M.
STEAMER	Oban......by Steamer Crinan............ ,,	8 0 10 0	RAIL	Oban............by Train Lochawe Station, ,,	8 5 9 4
"LINNET"	Crinan............ ,, Ardrishaig...... ,,	10 0 P.M. 12 15	"LOCHAWE"	Lochawe Pier.... ,, Ford............... ,,	9 5 10 40
COACH	Ardrishaig...... ,, Ford............... ,,	12 50 3 0	COACH	Ford............... ,, Ardrishaig........ ,,	10 45 P.M. 12 40
"LOCHAWE"	Ford............... ,, Lochawe Pier.... ,,	3 0 5 10	"LINNET"	Ardrishaig........ ,, Crinan............. ,,	1 0 2 55
RAIL	Lochawe Station, ,, Oban............... ,,	5 15 6 15	STR.	Crinan............. ,, Oban............... ,,	3 0 4 45

The times stated above are given merely for general information and are NOT guaranteed.

From Ardrishaig to Ford the route passes through the picturesque valley of Kilmartin and by Kilmartin Castle, Carnassarie Castle, Bull's Pass, Dog's Head Loch, and Ederline Loch. The attractions on Loch Awe are numerous. There are twenty-four islands, many of them richly wooded, and several crowned by the ruins of Castles and Monasteries. At the foot of the Lake is the romantic Pass of Brander, where MacDougall of Lorne encountered the Bruce, and where Ben Cruachan rises 3,800 feet from the Awe. For further description of route see pages 25 to 32 and 78 to 79.

OBAN to LOCH SUNART.
During Summer.
By Steamer "Pioneer."

Every Tuesday and Friday at 12-45 *p.m.; Returning every Wednesday and Saturday morning from Loch Sunart, or daily from Corran.*

CABIN RETURN FARE (Steamer only), 12s.

OBAN UP LOCHAWE
TO FORD AND BACK.
Daily during July, August and September.

By 8-5 a.m. Train from Oban to Lochawe Station, thence by Steamer "Lochawe" to Ford, returning by Steamer and Rail same evening.

Return Tickets issued at Oban Railway Station.
FIRST CLASS AND CABIN, 7s. 6d.; THIRD CLASS AND CABIN, 5s.

Starting by train for Lochawe, on leaving the station the line passes through the Drimamhargie cutting, and afterwards skirts the edge of Lochamhuillin—a low lying marshy flat—but which doubtless, ere many years elapse, and as Oban expands, will be filled up and built upon. As we sweep round to the left, and enter Glencruitten, many charming glimpses may be had of Oban Bay and its surroundings. After a continuous ascent for about three miles, the summit of the Glen is reached, and in a few minutes more a splendid panorama opens up to our gaze. The regal Dunstaffnage stands before us, still stately and grand in its ruins—the wooded peninsula on which it is built being washed by the quickly-flowing Etive; and on the other side of the loch are seen Benderloch, Beregonium, and the promontory of Lochnell, with the walls of its thrice-burnt and now renovated castle peeping above the tall trees that surround it. On our left is the modern mansion of the late Sir Donald Campbell (of Dunstaffnage). The famous Falls of Connel (or Lora) now comes in sight. The line now passes behind Kilmaronaig. Facing us on the other side is seen the large substantial parish church of Ardchattan, surrounded by a graveyard dotted by numerous tombstones, and considerable interest is attached to the mouldering ivy-mantled ruins of Ardchattan Priory, founded in the 14th century by an order of Cistercian monks. The mansion of Achnacloich, picturesquely situated on an eminence on our left is now conspicuous. Achnacloich and Taynuilt Stations are next passed, after which the River Nant is crossed, and speeding along by Bunawe passing on our left Inverawe House (Mrs. Cameron Campbell) we cross the River Awe and come to the Pass of Brander, where a good view can be had of the lofty Ben Cruachan. Lochawe Station is reached and the Steamer "Lochawe" is waiting to convey us to Ford at the south end of the lake, a distance of nearly thirty miles.* Three hours are given at Ford where passengers can ascend the famous Ben Dhu, and from the top of which on an ordinarily clear day a splendid view is to be had of Colonsay, Islay, Jura, Iona, and most of the western islands of Argyleshire.

* For description of scenery *on Lochawe*, see page 79.

GLASGOW TO INVERNESS & BACK,
(*VIA MULL OF KINTYRE*).
BY STEAM SHIPS
"CAVALIER" AND "STAFFA,"
With Goods and Passengers,
Every Monday and Thursday throughout the whole year.

CABIN FARE for the Round, with FIRST-CLASS SLEEPING ACCOMMODATION, 30s. ;
Or incluging MEALS, by Steamer leaving Glasgow on Monday, 60s. ; on Thursday, 65s.

The hours noted below are not to be absolutely relied upon—they only show about the average sailing time. The Steamer may be later than what is stated.

From	STAFFA. Monday.	CAVALIER. Thursday.	From	STAFFA. Thursday.	CAVALIER. Monday.
	a.m.	a.m.		a.m.	a.m.
Glasgow about	11 0	11 0	Inverness ab.	4 0	4 0
	p.m.	p.m.	Temple Pier ,,	5 45	5 45
Greenock ...,,	4 0	4 0	Inverfarigaig,,	6 15	6 15
	Tuesday.	Friday.	Foyers......,,	6 30	6 30
	a.m.	a.m.	Invermoriston.	7 0	7 0
Crinan......,,	3 30	3 30	Fort-Augustus	8 45	8 45
Craignish ...,,	4 0	4 0	Cullochy ....,,	9 30	9 30
Luing ......,,	4 30	4 30	Laggan .....,,	10 0	10 0
Easdale ....,,	5 15	5 15	Gairlochy ..,,	11 15	11 15
Oban ......,,	8 0	8 0		p.m.	p.m.
Appin ......,,	9 0	9 0	Banavie ....,,	2 15	2 15
Ballachulish.,,	10 15	10 15	Corpach ....,,	3 15	3 15
Corran......,,	11 0	11 0	Fort-William,,	6 0	6 0
Fort-William,,	3 0 p.	3 0 p.	Corran......,,	6 30	6 30
Corpach ....,,	4 0	4 0	Ballachulish ,.	7 0	7 0
	Wednesday	Saturday.	Appin ......,,	8 0	8 0
	a.m.	a.m.	Oban ....,,	10 0	10 0
Banavie ....,,	6 0	6 0	Easdale ....,,	11 0	11 0
Gairlochy ..,,	7 30	7 30	Luing ......,,	11 15	11 15
Laggan ....,,	9 0	9 0	Craignish ...,,	11 45	11 45
Cullochy ...,,	10 0	10 0	Crinan......,,	12 30	12 30
Fort-Augustus	12 0	12 0			
Invermoriston.	12 30 p.	12 30 p.		Friday.	Tuesday.
Foyers......,,	1 0	1 0	Greenock ...,,	Afternoon.	Afternoon.
Inverfarigaig,,	1 20	1 20			
TemplePier..,,	2 0	2 0	Glasgow ..arr.	Do.	Do.
Inverness arr.	4 0	4 0			

Tourists can obtain a pleasant trip by leaving Glasgow any Monday and Thursday at 11 A.M., or Greenock about 4 P.M. in the Splendid Screw Steamship "CAVALIER" or "STAFFA," for INVERNESS, Via MULL OF KINTYRE, going and returning through the SOUND OF JURA, LOCH

LINNHE, LOCHABER, and the CALEDONIAN CANAL, calling at OBAN, BALLACHULISH, FORT-WILLIAM, and Intermediate Places. The Route is through Scenery rich in historical interest and unequalled for grandeur and variety. In this way about a Week's most enjoyable Pleasure Sailing (sleeping on board the Steamer at night) may be had.

FOR DESCRIPTION OF ROUTE, SEE PAGES 28 to 53 INCLUSIVE.

BREAKFAST, DINNER, TEA, &c.,

SERVED IN FIRST CLASS STYLE

IN CABIN OF ALL THE STEAMERS,

(*With the exception of the "LINNET" on the Crinan Canal*)

At the undernoted Charges (including Steward's Fees):—

BREAKFAST, 2s.; *DINNER, 3s.; TEA (with meat) 2s.

*6d less on board the Glasgow & Ardrishaig and the Crinan & Oban Steamers,

---

In the "COLUMBA," "IONA," and other Swift Steamers, Meals are served IN FORE CABIN, at the undernoted Charges:—

(Including Steward's Fees).

BREAKFAST, 1/6; DINNER, 1/6; TEA (with Meat), 1/6.

A supply of Note Paper, Envelopes, Pens and Ink, is kept on the Writing Tables of each Steamer.

The foregoing is merely given for general information, and the Proprietor reserves the right of altering any of these arrangements at any time he may find it necessary.

A. SINCLAIR, PRINTER, 62 ARGYLE STREET, GLASGOW.

PIER MASTERS, FERRYMEN,
And Others Attending the Steamers, who are not Agents,
ON THE ROUTE OF
DAVID MACBRAYNE'S STEAMERS.

Aldourie, W. Findlay.
Appin, Alexander M'Lachlan.
Ardgour, John Smith.
Ardlamont, Peter Galbraith.
Arisaig, Donald Mackinnon.
Armadale, Peter Robertson.
Aultbea, Angus Stewart.
Ballachulish, William M'Donald.
Balmacara, Kenneth Mathieson.
Banavie, Ewen Mackinnon.
Bellanoch, Mrs. Brodie.
Black Mill Bay, Luing, L. M'Lachlan.
Broadford, John Ross.
Bruchladdich, John Thomson.
Carsaig, Archd. M'Fadyen.
Clachan, John M'Phail.
Colintraive, Andrew Turner.
Corpach, Ewen M'Kinnon.
Corran, John Smith.
Craignish, D. M'Farlane.
Craignure, Hector Currie.
Crinan, A. Cunningham.
Cullochy, Donald Williamson.
Dunmore, Hugh M'Kinnon.
Easdale, Archd. M'Kichan.
Eigg, Donald M'Leod.
Ford, D. Stewart.
Fort-Ausgustus, John Aitcheson.
Foyers, D. Elder.
Gairloch, A. Burgess.
Gairlochy, Robert M'Bride.

Gigha, John Smith.
Glenelg, Alexander M'Leod.
Harris, Angus M'Innes.
Inverfarigaig, David Kerr.
Inverie, A. Black.
Invermorriston, P. M'Donald.
Iona, John M'Donald.
Isleornsay, Neil Kennedy & Co.
Jura, Alex. M'Isaac.
Kilchoan, John Henderson.
Kyleakin, John Grant.
Laggan, John Fraser.
Lochaline, Archd. Graham.
Lochmaddy, M. M'Innes.
Luing, Lachlan M'Lachlan.
Plockton, D. & F. Matheson.
Poolewe, A. M'Lennon.
Port-Inisherrich, J. M'Lachlan.
Port-Sonnachan, T. Cameron.
Raasay, J. M'Millan.
Salen (Mull), Donald Fletcher.
Salen (Loch Sunart), D. Cameron.
Skipness, Alex. Thomson.
Staffa, John M'Donald.
Strome Ferry, James Baxter.
Tarbert, Harris, Angus M'Innes.
Temple Pier, J. Fraser.
Tighnabruaich, John Scoular.
Totaig, Loch Duich, R. Matheson.
Tychreggan, J. Munro.
Urquhart, J. Fraser.

HOTELS
ON THE ROUTE OF
DAVID MACBRAYNE'S STEAMERS.

Aldourie, 'Dores Inn,' 1½ miles.
Appin Hotel, Donald Carmichael.
Ardrishaig Hotel, John Finlay.
and Lorn Hotel, M. H. Prangnell,
Ardgour Hotel, John Smith.
Arisaig Hotel, M. Routledge.
Aultbea Hotel, Robert Forbes.
Ballachulish Hotel, John Currie.
Balmacara Hotel, Mrs. M'Leod.
Banavie, 'Locheil Arms,' J. Menzies.
Broadford Hotel, James Ross.
Bruchladdich Hotel, J. Thomson.
Cairnbaan Hotel, David Stevenson.
Carsaig,'Kinloch Hotel,' W. M'Donald
Clachan Inn, George Mathieson.
Colintraive Hotel, Andrew Turner.
Corpach Hotel, Colin M'Pherson.
Corran Hotel, John Smith.
Craignure Hotel, Hector Currie.
Crinan Inn, M. M'Callum.
Cullochy 'Invergarry Hotel,' J. M'Innes
Dunoon, Various Good Hotels.
Easdale Hotel, Mrs. Gillies.
Eigg Hotel, Donald MacLeod.
Ford, 'Achinellan Inn,' J. M'Dermaid.
Fort-Augustus, 'Lovat Arms,' M'Intosh
Fort-William, Various Good Hotels.
Foyers Hotel, D. Elder.
Gairloch Hotel, James Hornsby.
Gairlochy Inn, Mrs. M'Coll.
Gairlochy, 'Spean Bridge Hotel,' A. M'Donald (3 miles).
Gairlochy, 'Roy Bridge Hotel,' E. M'Intosh (6 miles).
Glenelg Hotel, Donald M'Intosh.
Greenock, 'Tontine Hotel,' Mrs. M'Dermott.
Harris Hotel, R. Hornsby.
Innellan, 'Royal Hotel,' John Clark.
Inveraray, 'Argyle' and 'George Hotel.'
Invermorriston Hotel, John M'Gregor.
Inverness, Various Good Hotels.
Iona, 'Columba Hotel,' George Ritchie.

Iona, 'Argyle Hotel,' J. Macdonald.
Isle Ornsay Hotel, John Nicolson.
Jura Hotel, John M'Kechnie.
Kilchoan Hotel, Dugald Black.
Kirn, 'Queen's Hotel,' Edw. Harding.
Kyleakin Hotel, Mrs. Turner.
Laggan, 'Invergarry Hotel,' J. M'Innes
Lochaline Hotels, A. Graham and Mrs. M'Innis.
Lochinver, Lochinver Hotel, John Dinnett.
Lochmaddy Hotel, M. M'Innis.
Oban, Numerous Splendid Hotels.
Plockton Inn, Henry Stewart.
Poolewe Hotel, A. M'Lennan.
Port-Askaig Hotel, Mrs. Bankier.
Port-Charlotte Hotel, Alexander Dick.
Port-Ellen, 'White Hart,' (M'Cuaig)
'Commercial,' (M'Leod).
Port-Inisherrich Inn, Mrs. M'Lachlan.
Portree, 'Royal,' (Ross) ; 'Portree Hotel,' (M'Innis) ; 'Caledonian,' (Murcheson);'Marine,'(Sutherland).
Port-Sonachan Hotel, T. Cameron.
Rothesay, Various Good Hotels.
Salen (Lochsunart) Hotel, D. Cameron.
Salen (Mull) Hotel, D. Campbell.
Skipness Hotel, Alex. Thomson.
Stornoway, 'Royal Hotel,' (M'Leod); 'Imperial,' (Cameron) ; 'Lewis,' (M'Dougall).
Strome Ferry,'Station Hotel,'J. Ross.
Strontian Hotel, John M'Lennan.
Tarbert (Lochfyne), M'Lean's Hotel.
do. Columba Hotel, J. M'Pherson.
Tarbert (Harris) Hotel, R. Hornsby.
Temple, 'Drumnadrochit,' J. Simpson.
Tighnabruaich,'Royal Hotel,(Duncan); 'Tighnabruaich Hotel,' (J. C. Lyle).
Tobermory, 'Western Isles Hotel.'
Tychreggan Hotel, J. & J. Munro.
Ullapool Hotel, Whyte.
Urquhart, 'Drumnadrochit,' J. Simpson

ENGLAND TO SCOTLAND AND BACK.

OBAN.

Holders of English Railway Companies'
EXCURSION TICKETS TO SCOTLAND
Will be booked on board the Royal Mail Steamer COLUMBA or IONA GLASGOW TO OBAN AND BACK FOR SINGLE FARE.

STEAMER RETURN.		CABIN	STEERAGE
CABIN. 13s. STEERAGE. 7s. 6d.	CIRCULAR TOUR { GOING BY STEAMER, RETURNING BY RAIL,	& 1st CLASS. 14s.	& 3rd CLASS. 8s.
CIRCULAR TOUR	{ GLASGOW to OBAN by Steamer and OBAN to EDINBURGH by Rail.	18s. 9d.	10s. 4d.

Return Tickets at Single Journey Fares are also issued from Edinburgh to Oban as under:—
From Princes Street (Cal. Rail) via Greenock and Crinan Canal.
From Waverley (N.B. Rail.) via Craigendoran, Dunoon, and Crinan Canal.
Return Fares, 1st Class and Cabin, 18/6; 3rd Class, and Steerage 9/10.
This arrangement applies only to *EXCURSIONS* from England throughout the Season.
FOR TOURIST FARES SEE PAGES 5, 6, AND 7.

The "Columba" or "Iona" sails from Glasgow daily at 7 a.m.

Circular Tourist Tickets in connection with the various Railways, are issued on board the

"COLUMBA" or "IONA."

The undernoted Railway Companies book Tourists from London, Liverpool, Manchester, Birmingham, Preston, York, Newcastle, Sheffield, Leeds, Bradford, Carlisle, Dumfries, Edinburgh, Glasgow, &c., to Oban, and the West Highlands, by DAVID MACBRAYNE'S Royal Mail Steamers.

LONDON AND NORTH WESTERN AND CALEDONIAN RAILWAYS.	} WEST COAST ROUTE.
THE MIDLAND AND GLASGOW AND SOUTH WESTERN RAILWAYS.	} MIDLAND ROUTE.
GREAT NORTHERN, NORTH EASTERN, AND NORTH BRITISH RAILWAYS.	} EAST COAST ROUTE.

LANCASHIRE AND YORKSHIRE RAILWAY.
MANCHESTER, SHEFFIELD, & LINCOLNSHIRE RAILWAY,
LONDON AND SOUTH WESTERN RAILWAY,
GREAT EASTERN RAILWAY,
GREAT WESTERN RAILWAY,
GREAT NORTH OF SCOTLAND RAILWAY,
AND HIGHLAND RAILWAY.

Tourist Tickets in connection with David MacBrayne's Steamers, are issued throughout England at the various offices of Thomas Cook & Son; Henry Gaze & Son; Swan & Leach, Ltd; Dawson & Dean, and John Frame, Tourist and Excursion Agents; and by R. H. V. Wragge, Tourist Agent, 26 Coney St., York.

Time Bill, Map and List of Fares sent free on application to the Owner,

DAVID MACBRAYNE, 119 HOPE STREET, GLASGOW.

AGENTS FOR STEAMERS.

WM. LINDSAY & Co., Highland Steamers, ...*Greenock.*
JOHN DAWSON, Lochfyne and Islay Steamers, ...*Greenock.*
F. BROWN ....*Kirn.*
WILLIAM MATON ....*Dunoon*
A. M'KELLAR ....*Innellan.*
ROBERT WATSON ....*Rothesay.*
JAMES TULLOCH ....*Tarbert.*
ALEXANDER MACDONALD ....*Ardrishaig.*
ALEXANDER BROWN ....*Oban.*
JOHN MURDOCH ....*Fort-William.*
JOHN MACKINTOSH ....*Inverness.*
WALTER MALCOLM ....*Inveraray.*
LACHLAN M'CUAIG ....*Port-Ellen.*
MALCOLM BELL ....*Port-Askaig.*
JOHN MASSON ....*Tobermory.*
DONALD MACDONALD ....*Portree.*
JOHN HARROLD ....*Stornoway.*
KENNETH CAMERON ....*Ullapool.*
JAMES GORDON ....*Lochinver.*

OFFICIAL GUIDE BOOK, 3d. ; ILLUSTRATED, 6d. ; CLOTH GILT, 1s.
To be had at Railway Bookstalls throughout England and Scotland, on board all the Steamers, from Agents for Steamers, and from the Owner,

TELEGRAPHIC ADDRESS,
"MACBRAYNE, GLASGOW."

DAVID MACBRAYNE,
119 HOPE STREET, GLASGOW.

TOURISTS SPECIAL CABIN TICKETS

Issued during the Season,

Giving the privilege of the run of all the undernoted Steamers to any part of the Highlands at which they may call during the time specified.

One Week, £3; Two Weeks, £5; Or, Six Separate Days, £3 10s.

"GRENADIER" New Royal Mail Steamship.

	CAPTAIN.	PURSER.
With Passengers only.		
COLUMBA	Capt. M'Gaw,	Mr. Alex. Paterson.
IONA	„ A. Campbell,	„ W. S. M'Donald.
CHEVALIER ...	„ J. M'Millan,	„ J. J. Lawson.
MOUNTAINEER ...	„ D. M'Callum,	„ J. C. Orrock.
PIONEER	„ J. M'Callum,	„ J. Black.
GLENCOE	„ A. Baxter,	„ H. MacKay.
GONDOLIER	„ J. M'Kechnie,	„ A. Archibald.
GLENGARRY ...	„ J. Carmichael,	„ T. Fraser.
LOCHAWE	„ Jn. Carmichael,	„ J. M'Innes.
LINNET	„ D. M'Callum,	„ Lawson.
With Goods and Passengers.		
CLAYMORE	„ M. M'Neill,	„ J. L. Masson
CLANSMAN	„ M. Sinclair,	„ S. Young.
CLYDESDALE ...	„ A. M'Callum,	„ J. Lamb.
CAVALIER	„ M'Tavish,	„ D. M'Pherson
STAFFA	„ A. M'Kinnon,	„ D. H. Dewar.
ISLAY	„ J. M'Neill,	„ G. M'Kenzie.
LOCHNESS ...	„ D. Cameron,	„ D. Williamson.
LOCHIEL	„ D. M'Nab,	„ Wardrop.
FINGAL	„ A. Campbell,	„ Campbell.
ETHEL	„ D. M'Tavish,	„ K. Macaskill.
INVERARAY CASTLE	„ N. M'Tavish,	„ J. Lang.

www.ingramcontent.com/pod-product-compliance
Lightning Source LLC
Chambersburg PA
CBHW020058170426
43199CB00009B/318